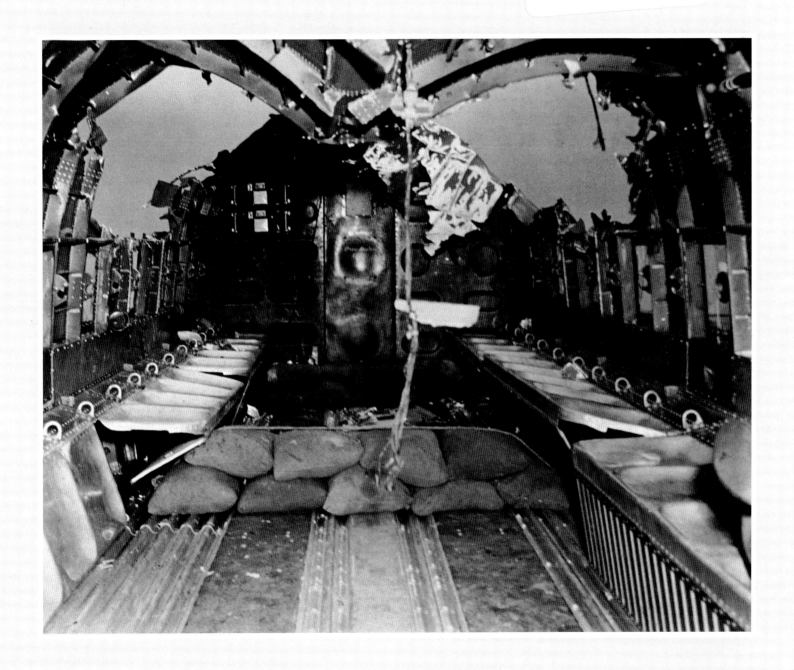

SHOT TO HELL

THE STORIES AND PHOTOS OF RAVAGED WWII WARBIRDS

CORY GRAFF

MBI

This edition first published in 2003 by MBI Publishing Company, Galtier Plaza, Suite 200, 380 Jackson Street, St. Paul, MN 55101-3885 USA

© Cory Graff, 2003

MBI Publishing Company titles are also available at discounts in bulk quantity for industrial or sales-promotional use. For details write to Special Sales Manager at Motorbooks International Wholesalers & Distributors, Galtier Plaza, Suite 200, 380 Jackson Street, St. Paul, MN 55101-3885 USA.

ISBN 0-7603-1609-0

On the front cover: Army Air Forces ground crewmen bravely fight to douse a burning Republic P-47 Thunderbolt with flame-smothering foam. The aircraft was headed to the front lines in support of Allied troops in France when it was involved in a takeoff accident on June 21, 1944—just two weeks after D-Day. *National Archives/Army Air Forces*

On the frontispiece: After riddling a 1st Troop Carrier Group C-47 with ammunition, a frustrated Japanese fighter pilot decided to crash into the escaping plane. But the sturdy cargo craft flew on and safely landed, even though its fuselage was blown wide open. *The Boeing Company Archives*

On the title page: This L-4A, slyly named *The Pie-Eyed Piper*, has seen better days. Most everything that could be used on another aircraft has been stripped away from the plane that crashed in a Manila airfield. *Military History Institute/Russo Collection*

Table of Contents: *Republic Aviation News* ran this image of a battle-ravaged P-47 as a tribute to the toughness of the Jug on July 23, 1943. It reportedly was pounded by five 20mm shells from an attacking German fighter over enemy territory. After a rough landing in England, Lieutenant Justus Foster walked away from the battered fighter unharmed. *National Archives/Army Air Forces*

On the back cover: Small parts and pieces of aircraft were as good as gold at far-from-home airfields. Here, soldiers from a salvage depot pick over the wreckage of a B-17 hit in a bombing raid on January 9, 1943 in North Africa. *Military History Institute/Milne Collection*

About the author
Cory Graff is the exhibits research and development manager at The Museum of Flight in Seattle, Washington. He currently is in charge of creating an exhibit about World War I fighter aviation, which will cover 25,000 square feet and contain 18 aircraft. Another of Cory's exhibits, created for the Frye Art Museum, detailed the story of a XB-29 crash in Seattle in 1943. In his free time, he works on other aviation-related projects, including writing and conducting research. One of his articles covering the battered aircraft of World War II was published in the Smithsonian's *Air & Space* magazine. *Shot to Hell: The Stories and Photos of Ravaged WWII Warbirds* is his first book.

Edited by Steve Gansen and Leah Cochenet Noel
Designed by Russ Kuepper

Printed in China

Table of Contents

Preface

It must have been the thrill of a lifetime—perhaps the thrill of a thousand lifetimes. A year before, he was just a boy, in school, in Nowhere, America. Today, the same boy, now at the ripe old age of 22, was in command of a beautiful silver six-ton fighter plane racing over the final yards of the English Channel and into enemy territory. But with the thrill of a lifetime came responsibility. On this day, the job demanded that he and his companions slow their sleek machines to a painfully slow zigzagging crawl, pick up a group of heavy bombers, and shepherd them into Germany.

With the thrill came danger, too. There were bound to be enemy fighters, maybe in the hands of veterans with years of air-combat experience—German men who would fight like hell to protect their land, hometowns, and their families. Or maybe he'd stumble across these new German jets he'd heard about and get a crack at one.

The thought of enemy fighters makes him sit a little straighter in his seat, glance in the rearview mirror, and then turn his body around to get a good look out the back of his bubble canopy. He'd done it thousands of times—looking for enemy fighters—and his neck was rubbed raw from chafing against his parachute straps. He sure as hell wasn't going to let one of those new jets get a crack at him.

Today, there most definitely would be flak. There always was, pounding the skies and randomly picking a bomber from the large formation and ripping it in two. Another bomber lurched to one side and then started to roll over, as if in slow motion. Good God, he was so glad he wasn't one of the boys in those bombers, tumbling out into the cold air at 30,000 feet, clawing for his ripcord.

Once, he'd picked up a straggler on the way home. He'd been hounding a train when his wingman noticed a speck near the horizon, coming their way. It was a Boeing Flying Fortress, all alone. As his plane moved closer to the bomber, he could see that it was in trouble. Pulling his Mustang in beside the lumbering wreck, he could hardly believe his eyes. The nose was gone, peeled back, and ripped away to the cockpit. The bomber must have caught an antiaircraft shell squarely in the snout. The bombardier's empty chair swiveled in the wreckage, and the plane's nose guns chattered in the wind.

A half hearted wave from the "flight" engineer aboard the B-17 was the only sign of life he could see from the cockpit. He imagined the two pilots struggling to keep their machine under control. He wondered if they could make it home and how they could stand the cold air thundering through the gaping hole in the nose. He wondered if they had families. Then he checked the skies again for fighters.

As the low-flying bomber slowly moved over the landscape headed for the sea, it collected gunshots from the towns below. One of the frustrated waist gunners answered back with a blast from his .50-

caliber gun. Even if the crippled bomber did make the miraculous flight all the way back to England, there was no way to know if the landing gear would come down or if the pilots could keep control of the big bomber. There were no guarantees any of them would be alive to fly again tomorrow.

The boy's Mustang was running low on fuel. He wouldn't be able to stick with the bomber, so he and his wingman simply waggled their wings and pulled away, leaving the straggler alone again on the long journey to safety. He opened the throttle and dove toward the deck. As he crossed over the beach and out into the Channel once more, he wondered if the boys in the crippled Fortress would make it. And, if they made it today, would they ever make it back to America? Back to their wives, and mothers, and homes? Then, he wondered if he'd live to see Nowhere, America, again.*

*Note: This preface is based on a few sentences found in the 398th Bomb Group history printed by Vanguard Press, in which B-17 pilot Larry DeLancey describes bringing his heavily damaged plane back to England from a mission over Cologne on October 15, 1944. He says, "About this time a pair of P-51s showed up and flew a loose formation on us across Belgium. I often wondered what they thought as they looked at the mess up front."

Acknowledgments

I would like to thank the following people and institutions for their assistance in the creation of this book: Jay Graybeal at the Military History Institute at Carlisle Barracks in Pennsylvania, who admitted that he was delighted to take a short break from Civil War research; the people at the National Archives Still Picture Branch, who brought me an endless stream of the army's images; Dennis Case and the helpful people at the Air Force Historical Research Agency at Maxwell Air Force Base in Alabama for showing me many unique shots and sharing the history behind them. Thanks also go to Katherine Williams, John Little, Dennis Parks, Richard Beckerman, Addy Froehlich, and Janice Baker at The Museum of Flight—a unique institution for scholarly aviation research—and to Mike Lombardi, Pat McGinniss, and Tom Lubbesmeyer at The Boeing Company Historical Archives. Alan Renga at the San Diego Aerospace Museum quickly cruised through the museum's great photograph collection for me. Brett Stolle at the U.S. Air Force Museum gladly helped me with some strange questions. Stan Piet at the Glenn L. Martin Aviation Museum graciously allowed me to view his personal collection. Peter Bowers, Kenneth Sumney, Ralph Burbridge, and Bill Agee donated images for the creation of this book. Judy and Gary Graff, mom and dad, thanks! Thanks also to Sean and Katherine Martin and to Jean Churchill. And thanks to Steve Gansen, Leah Noel, and Jennifer Boxmeyer at MBI Publishing Company.

An army flyer snapped this dramatic photograph of a falling Martin B-26 Marauder somewhere over Occupied Europe. Flames or gunfire have separated the cowling from the port engine, and the fire has burned through the fabric-covered control surfaces on the tail. *National Archives/Army Air Forces*

Flirting with Death

Danger was an ever-present companion to the combat flyer in World War II. From the fighter pilots who struggled into the air during he Japanese attack on Pearl Harbor to the bomber crewmen who dutifully flew supply missions to prisoner of war camps after the fighting had ceased, risk was a way of life in the Army Air Forces (AAF). Accidents, injury, and death were simply part of the deal—part of the job of flying high-performance fighting machines under wartime conditions.

In the conflict that would become known as The Great War—World War I—an airman could expect to live an appallingly brief six to eight weeks while flying an airplane in combat. One of the most famous American aces, Frank Luke, lived 17 days from the time of his first official victory to the day he was killed in France. For the men who flew in the fighters, bombers, and cargo planes during World War II, the odds were a bit better but still frightening.

Whether in the high-risk business of flying bomber raids into Germany, mixing it up with Japanese fighters above the Pacific, or hauling fuel and ammunition over the Himalayas, avoiding death wasn't always a matter of skill. Flak randomly chose an unlucky soul and ended his life in a shower of shredded metal and greasy black smoke. When an enemy fighter pilot arrived at the right place and the right time—or the terrible weather closed in leaving nowhere to go but down—an American flyer never had a chance.

In early 1944, for example, U.S. bomber crewmen based in England often forgot about their need to survive 25 missions after they had flown on a few. After seeing the confused and grisly high-stakes game of Russian roulette that took place almost every day over Germany and Occupied Europe, an airman prophesied that there was a bullet with his name on it out there, somewhere, just waiting to get him or kill him indirectly by incapacitating his airplane. "The

Armorers of the 405th Fighter Group remove .50-caliber ammunition from the gun bays of a severely damaged P-47D. Note that the bare metal canopy from another airplane has been installed on the fighter. *The Museum of Flight/Army Air Forces*

Golden BB," as some flyers called it, might be an antiaircraft shell that was, at that moment, being transported by truck to an air-defense battery near Cologne or a 30mm cannon round being slipped into a long belt of identical shells at an ammunition factory in Hamburg. An airman couldn't avoid it—he really had no idea exactly what his fate was or where it lie, only that when the time came, he and "the BB" were destined to meet at exactly the same place and at the same time in the massive expanse of sky.

Army officials found that it wasn't only the monumental air battle with enemy forces that could erase the name of a good flyer from the squadron's roster. Losses happened as an understandable part of routine military activities, such as a takeoff accident in a heavily loaded fighter or a collision with another bomber while searching for the formation in the early-morning haze. It was a proven fact that a fatigued pilot could, in the simple act of flipping the wrong switch, set off a series of events that could easily land a dozen army airmen in a prison camp, adrift at sea, or worse.

"Gremlins," as Allied airmen called them, could destroy a plane and its pilot with ease. These imaginary, gnomelike creatures created mechanical problems in aircraft and were a mythical part of British and, later, U.S. aviation life. A British ditty of the time says:

> White ones will wiggle your wing tips,
> Male ones will muddle your maps,
> Green ones will guzzle your glycol,
> Females will flutter your flaps.
> Pink ones will perch on your Perspex,
> And dance pirouettes on your prop,
> There's a spherical middle-aged gremlin,
> Who'll spin on your stick like a top.

While the creatures may not have been believable, the malfunctions and failures that they supposedly delighted in making were very real and could kill a flyer.

Then there were other accidents that defied logic and left the army brass fuming. Besides the obvious dangers of enemy fighters, flak, or pesky gremlins, the American airman, forever ingenious, found hundreds of other ways to do himself in. From the first days of pilot training, the warnings were shot out rapid-fire: "Never turn too low. Don't ever overstress the airplane. Don't get lost. Be aware of those flying around you. Don't ever panic, buster. And never, ever be a showoff—graveyards are filled with 'em." Some trainees dutifully listened, went through months of expensive and risky flight training, were shipped overseas, and then did something silly, like walk into a spinning propeller. Another classic example of stupidity that left commanders speechless was when an army pilot flew to the town of an English girl he'd met and plowed his P-51 through her front door with an impressive, but alas, slightly *too* low, low pass.

In wartime publications, army leadership constantly reminded airmen to be smart and careful. "The Keystone Cops are funny in the movies," General Hap Arnold said in one such safety newsletter. "But the AAF has no place for GI jokers on its flight lines. Carelessness breeds avoidable accidents, delays training, and lengthens the war." The last part got many soldiers to listen—they wanted to go home.

Luckily, printed matter doesn't convey sound—this must have been an ugly one. This P-38G developed a shimmy in the nose wheel when taxiing for takeoff on February 1, 1944. When the vibration continued, the pilot knew that "gremlins" had canceled his mission, and he turned around. Before he could return to his parking spot, the nose wheel sheared off where the strut joins the strut cylinder. *Air Force Historical Research Agency*

The general continued with some advice: "To commanders: Weed out the incompetent and weak, eliminate the disobedient, discipline the careless, retain hard, fearless, and disciplined men. To pilots: Self-discipline makes men—unafraid to fight, die, or turn back. Let the enemy see your bravery. The Air Forces know of it! To crews, mechanics, and sentinels on guard: Only through your efforts can this job be done. To every man in the Air Forces, I pass these words: The responsibility is yours, the job is yours. Do it."

A flyer's education about how to stay alive happened in less heavy-handed ways, too. When not talking about women or liquor, airmen spent many of their stressful hours between missions telling stories about flight. They all loved a good flying story. Some of the best, it seemed, dealt with crashes, accidents, and combat. There was certainly a fascination with the subject, and with good reason.

Army pilots were eager to learn from another man's mistakes and experiences. Almost every good flying yarn held a lesson or a moral. Among his peers, a flyer could laugh as he told about the knucklehead who rigged his control cables backward. He was free to talk about "how funny it was" when he pinched off his own oxygen supply, as long as he was telling it to those who understood the situation. Or he could have his fellow pilots rolling on the floor as he related the "hilarious time" that the bombs hung up in the lead bomber, causing him to risk his ass over the flak-blasted target not once, not twice, but *three* times. The stories were entertaining, to be sure, but they

Army ground personnel work carefully to right a Beech UC-43 Traveler at Wright Field, Ohio. While the pilot of this plane tried to cross behind a B-24 Liberator, an engineer in the cockpit of the big bomber ran up to the engines and blew the Beech over onto its nose on July 19, 1944. *Air Force Historical Research Agency*

A Waco CG-4A swoops in low for landing during the army's Carolina maneuvers on May 25, 1943. Note the pilot's control inputs, apparent from the position of the elevator and ailerons, to correct the dangerous bank and bring the glider down safely. His efforts may have been too little, too late, though, to avoid a really rough landing. *National Archives/Army Air Forces*

were talk of lessons learned, corners into which pilots had unknowingly painted themselves into only to make a miraculous escape.

Other times, there was more serious talk about those who didn't make it. Ideas and theories came out as to what might have gone wrong, what could have been done differently, and, perhaps, speculation as to what the surviving airmen might have attempted to do if they found themselves in a similar situation. Sobering talk about what to do (and what not to do) when, say, a P-38 Lightning's engine dies on takeoff, could make a pilot more prepared for the day it happened to him.

Regardless of the type of accident or battle damage that led to a crash, once a plane had settled to earth, the ground crews stepped in. It was said during World War II that, for every man in the army who flew, there were nine men on the ground who kept him supplied and looked after his plane. Depending on where an aircraft came down and its condition, the first task was to determine whether the plane would ever fly again.

Damage on a California flight line would be treated differently than similar damage in New Guinea, according to the availability of parts, other airplanes, and repair facilities. An article about combat in Australia noted that, "airplane parts which have made the long sea trip from America are worth more than diamonds here." A service squadron based in Australia traveled for miles to get to the wreck of a smashed P-40 that belly-landed into the dense jungle. A similar P-51 wreck in England might be sent to the salvage dump almost immediately with the knowledge that another Mustang would be arriving soon.

Aircraft that could not be repaired economically were dubbed Category E; they were stricken from the records and any usable parts were stripped off for use on other craft. Some of the most interesting examples of this swapping of parts can be seen on Eighth Air Force bombers. Photographs reveal olive drab–painted cowlings, outer wing panels, or other parts from a long-gone Boeing B-17 that have been installed on a newer, bare-metal Flying Fortress. In some cases, the good halves of two planes were grafted together to make one flyable bomber. The men of the Army Air Forces were interested in practical, not pretty, solutions in order to keep as many planes as possible in flying shape.

Some Category E planes also had a knack for coming back to life. A B-25 Mitchell that was almost totally destroyed in New Guinea was given the "thumbs down" by inspectors. One of them commented that not even the North American Aviation Company factory itself would be able to repair it. Squadron mechanics knew, in those early days of the war, that these bombers weren't exactly plentiful in the Pacific, so the mechanics went about performing a resurrection anyway. Renamed *Patches* (what else?), the Frankenstein-like B-25 carried parts from perhaps 10 other wrecks. It took three months to get the bomber back into the air and fighting the Japanese.

Sometimes, aircraft coming home from a mission with serious damage were even directed to fly to an air depot instead of returning to base, especially if a belly landing looked unavoidable. At the depot, the plane could be raised back onto its gear, patched up, and sent back into battle with efficiency. Planes that were less lucky and more damaged could be made into skeletons quickly and cut into pieces with acetylene torches with similar speed. What used to be an airplane was recycled for the valuable metal it contained, which rapidly was made into new aircraft parts.

One classic story of the scrap pile involves an "eager beaver" in the southwest Pacific who misunderstood a visiting general's request. When the general gave the order to make the stockpile of damaged planes "nice and orderly," the all-too-cooperative soldier misinterpreted the offhanded comment and converted the planes into a single, neat bundle with the use of a bulldozer. The 20-foot pile contained dozens of aircraft and cost the U.S. Army thousands of dollars in destroyed parts.

Other AAF repair crews were mobile, heading out to any area where a plane might have come down. In one instance, a bomber named *Sir Baboon McGoon* of the 91st Bomb Group belly-landed at a muddy British fighter field. A mobile repair unit came to the scene and raised the Fortress onto its gear with inflatable balloon jacks. Next, the unit changed out damaged propellers and engines and patched up the crushed chin and ball turrets. While this work was underway, an engineering unit was busy filling in ditches and laying down steel matting for the plane's takeoff. (The landing in soft mud was an advantage on the way into the field, but now it threatened to keep the big aircraft mired there for good.) Days later, the bomber was airborne and on its way for more extensive repairs

Balloon jacks were used to lift aircraft back onto their gear after a belly landing. The "go anywhere" air bags could lift up to 12 tons. Here, one of the inflatable "pillows" is demonstrated at Wright Field in Ohio. *Author's collection*

while the mobile repair crew stenciled the silhouette of another rescued plane on the side of the trailer that they used as a mobile workshop.

Of course, in addition to mobile repair units, men at each air base cared for the planes, too. Amid usually primitive conditions, mechanics struggled day and night to keep aircraft in airworthy condition and make modifications and repairs. In England, endless cold, wet, and dreary nights kept these airmen company as they performed constant engine changes and patched plenty of holes. In Alaska, it was always either freezing or a muddy mess, depending on the season. The bases in the Pacific were less than a tropical paradise, with blazing heat, bugs, an occasional Japanese attack, and, perhaps most frustrating, an often agonizingly slow supply line of spare parts from the United States. North Africa brought storms that sandblasted planes and fouled mechanical parts and engines, which made it very tough to get any repairs or maintenance accomplished. These AAF men worked miracles to get hundreds of combat planes back into the air, yet hardly ever received any credit.

Another job that the men at air bases did regularly was rescue work, including firefighting and caring for the wounded airmen returning from combat. Ground crewmen saw more than their fair share of drama as they counted planes coming back from a mission. Bombers sometimes limped miles and miles back from Germany only to be turned into heaps of burning wreckage right before the ground crewmen's eyes. Others hastily

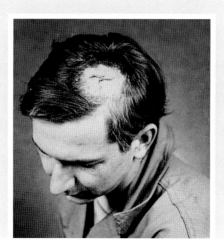

A flyer from the 448th Bomb Group displays his flak-wounded head. This photo was taken on May 2, 1944. *Air Force Historical Research Agency*

Ground crewmen give an injured gunner plasma as the flyer's crashed B-26 Marauder burns in the background. This image was taken in England in mid-1944. *National Archives/Army Air Forces*

came straight in, firing a red flare as they landed, signaling "wounded aboard." And still others slid to a stop, battered and broken, as the men on the ground pumped gallons of fire-smothering foam on smoldering engines.

Some wounded men were carried out of the planes on stretchers, while other, luckier flyers were left to ogle over the holes made in flak vests and helmets. Covering the chest and abdomen, a flak vest was considered heavy and uncomfortable by many army airmen, but, as one bomber flyer commented, "It gets lighter with every mile you go inside enemy territory until finally you wonder if it is heavy enough to do the job!"

Ritual-like, it was customary for those who came through a mission unscathed to set foot on Mother Earth and then, almost immediately, circle the plane, looking for holes and damage. Partly amused and partially amazed, a tail gunner would point out a hole ripped by a 30mm cannon shell just inches from where his head had been. Or a pilot would gasp as he realized that the reason he had no yaw control as he returned from Germany was that his rudder hadn't come home with the rest of the ship.

It seems like someone was there with a camera almost without fail, snapping shots of holes, dents, or even the jumble of scorched parts that remained after the action. Men captured images of the ground crews trying to figure out what it would take to get the plane back into shape or even back onto solid ground. A plane wreck was somewhat like a car wreck—everyone came to take a look, even if they really didn't want to. Also captured on film were the grim faces of those who had cheated death once again, intermixed with the smiles of relief and the clowning poses for the newspapers and the folks back home.

This book is a collection of these amazing images. It gives the reader a unique glimpse into the dangerous lives of army airmen who flew the planes of World War II. Gathered from government institutions, veteran flyers, and private collectors, this publication contains one of the largest and most comprehensive accounts of battle damage and aircraft accidents of army aircraft from the World War II era, with photos from the major theaters of war—Europe and the Pacific—and also from far-away airfields in Iceland, Calcutta, and the Aleutians. Along with the images are the stories behind the photos, covering every kind of plane, from heavy bombers desperately fighting to stay in the air to the troop-filled assault gliders. Enjoy the adventure, and be careful up there.

A pair of Flying Fortress crewmen look through the holed wingtip of their bomber. The B-17 became legendary for its ability to return home with terrible damage. *National Archives/Army Air Forces*

Chapter 1

Heavy Bombers

The prototype Boeing 299's tail surfaces were spared from fire after it crashed at Wright Field on October 30, 1935. Two out of the five men aboard the plane—the chief of Wright Field's flight testing section, Ployer Hill, and Boeing's chief pilot, Leslie Tower—died from injuries suffered in the accident. Investigators quickly found the problem: the control surfaces on the tail were locked, as they were supposed to be while the aircraft was parked on the ground. *The Museum of Flight/Army Air Forces*

Unbreakable Fortress

The B-17 Flying Fortress was built to be tough. From the bomber's beginnings, the Boeing Airplane Company's president, Clairmont Egtvedt, envisioned a big machine as "an aerial battleship." When the B-17, called Project 299, was rolled out for the public to view in July 1935, an impressed *Seattle Times* newsman wrote that the giant aircraft was a "flying fortress."

During army evaluations at Wright Field in October 1935, the 299 crashed on takeoff. Investigators found that no one had remembered to unlock the tail control surfaces, which were held immobile while the plane was parked on the ground. Though the crash was not the fault of the designers, some critics in the Air Corps protested that the large bomber was "too much airplane for a pilot to handle." But there were advocates of the Flying Fortress too, and modest numbers of the plane began to roll off the assembly line.

At the outbreak of war, the B-17 served with distinction in North Africa and the Pacific. On February 1, 1943, a B-17 named *All American* survived a terrible collision with a German Bf 109 fighter and continued to fly. On the 90-minute ride to safety, a crewman in another Fortress snapped a photograph of the stricken bomber, with a horrible gash through its tail and its horizontal stabilizer completely missing. The image was used by Boeing in advertisements, above the headline, "No Achilles Heel." The legend of the Flying Fortress had begun.

As the bombing campaign in Europe geared up, Boeing, Douglas, and Lockheed-Vega factories in the United States churned out B-17s day and night. When found to be vulnerable to head-on runs from enemy fighters, later models of the Fortress came from the factory with an ugly but effective chin turret to discourage such bold attacks.

On bombing missions, B-17s sometimes suffered unbelievable damage yet managed to stay in the air. With its engines blasted, tail torn apart, or the fuselage ripped open, the brawny bomber had an almost supernatural will to keep flying. It has been suggested that some all-metal aircraft that were created when the concept was fairly new— such as the Douglas DC-3 and Boeing B-17—were over-engineered by unsure designers. That was certainly fine with Flying Fortress airmen, who felt they flew an exceptional machine through the hellish flak and fighters over the target. Though the legend of the Flying Fortress has taken on mythic proportions, it is important to note that nearly 40 percent of the seemingly unstoppable B-17s sent to Europe never made it home.

The Winsome Winn of the 381st Bomb Group pulls off the target with an engine smoking on October 12, 1943. The grizzled veteran Boeing B-17F Flying Fortress was lost in January 1944 on a raid over Germany. Eight men aboard the bomber were captured and two flyers were killed. *National Archives/Army Air Forces*

Little Miss Mischief of the 91st Bomb Group was on a mission over Cologne, Germany, on October 15, 1944, when she was hit by an antiaircraft shell. With two injured gunners, the plane dropped from formation and turned toward home. Pilot Paul McDowell and engineer James Hobbs (seen on the right inspecting *Miss Mischief*'s damage) worked together to fly the plane, with Hobbs pulling on the severed rudder and trim tab cables at McDowell's request. After landing, the Lockheed-Vega–built B-17G's belly damage was judged too great to be repaired economically. The blasted tail section was removed from the plane at the production break, and a "new used" one from a cannibalized Boeing-built Flying Fortress was installed in its place. The strange results can be seen in the photograph (below). With a half olive drab and gray and half natural metal finish, this veteran of 50 missions crash-landed on April 4, 1945. Note the feathered outboard propeller. *National Archives/Army Air Forces*

This famous photo was taken after the same Cologne raid in which *Little Miss Mischief* was injured. Larry DeLancey's B-17G of the 398th Bomb Group took an 88mm shell though the nose right over the target. Everything in the nose was devastated—instruments, oxygen, communications, and hydraulics. However, the engines were still running and the controls seemed operable, so DeLancey turned west and dove down to 2,000 feet as he retreated toward the English Channel. In a magnificent feat of navigation and bravery, DeLancey and his crew nursed the Flying Fortress to its home base of Nuthampstead, England. *National Archives/Army Air Forces*

Sweet Pea of the 2nd Bomb Group was hit over Debreczen, Hungary, on September 21, 1944. The squadron's history claims, "A hole large enough for a jeep to pass through was blasted into the side of the Fortress, almost severing the huge craft in two." After viewing the damage, crews in surrounding B-17s in the formation immediately gave up all hope of ever seeing *Sweet Pea* again. But after 520 miles of flying, the Fortress returned to Foggia, Italy, its tail collapsing to the ground during landing. A *Boeing News Weekly* article written after the miraculous return claimed the tail was held in place "by a few longitudinals and 27 inches of skin." *National Archives/Army Air Forces*

An attacking Bf 109 fighter tumbled through the tail of a 97th Bomb Group B-17F named *All American* on a mission to Tunis, Tunisia, on February 1, 1943. Flyers in other B-17s were astonished to see the stricken bomber pitch up, recover, and keep flying. An airman aboard *The Flying Flint Gun* snapped a photograph that would become famous. It shows *All American* struggling to make it home with no port horizontal stabilizer and a terrible gash through the fuselage. The photo was sent home with the following message: "Censor, Should there be some law, rule, or regulation against sending the picture below to my wife, please seal the flap above and return—it is an unduplicateable [*sic*] shot and one I should hate to lose." *All American* made it back to Biskra, Algeria, with all aboard safe. *National Archives/Army Air Forces*

An aerial view of the 95th Bomb Group's base in Alconbury, England, on May 27, 1943. It shows a number of B-17s near where one Flying Fortress was blown to pieces while 10 500-pound bombs were loaded onboard. Eleven aircraft were damaged by the blast, and 19 men were killed and 20 others injured. *National Archives/Army Air Forces*

Over Cologne, Germany, on September 27, 1944, this Flying Fortress caught a flak shell squarely in the ball turret at altitude. The ball turret gunner and radio operator were blown out of the ship, and an amazingly large section of the starboard side of the fuselage was blasted open. "Somehow, the plane held together," the 351st Bomb Group's history notes, and the pilot was able to bring the B-17 back for a landing at Polebrook, England. *National Archives/Army Air Forces*

The 379th Bomb Group lost three B-17s when it was attacked by 75 enemy fighters on a mission to Berlin, Germany, on May 24, 1944. While two of the bombers were shot down by attacking aircraft, the third aircraft remained unaccounted for. The group's history states that "the other was either hit by fighters or possibly had a collision with a fighter or with one of our planes." The latter seems most likely when viewing the damage to this 379th aircraft that made it back to Kimbolton, England, on the same day. *National Archives/Army Air Forces*

This Flying Fortress of the 305th Bomb Group returned to Chelveston, England, after a mission that was called off due to poor weather on August 29, 1943. While testing a new carburetor on the No. 4 engine, the plane caught fire. For an hour, crewmen and fire personnel fought to get the blazing aircraft, fully loaded with bombs, under control. Finally, brave men started the ship and taxied it away from other bombers parked nearby. No one was hurt when the Fortress blew apart. *National Archives/Army Air Forces*

One can imagine the foul language and frustrated outbursts that must have echoed down the flight line after this accident. These two new B-17Gs were fresh out of Boeing's Plant Two in Seattle, when they met in a taxiing accident. At the height of production, Boeing's Seattle plant was building 16 heavy bombers each day. It is unknown whether these B-17s were repaired or simply scrapped. *Peter Bowers Collection*

A crewman looks over the extensive damage to *Little Miss Mischief*, a B-17G of the 91st Bomb Group on April 4, 1945. Parts, like the forward hatch and cockpit windows, have already been removed for use on other planes. During the belly landing, the Fort's chin turret was forced back into the fuselage—a common occurrence on late-model B-17s. *National Archives/Army Air Forces*

Flyers look over a 20mm hole blasted through the port wing of the B-17G dubbed *The Peacemaker*. On a mission to Leipzig, Germany, on July 20, 1944, the bomber was pounced on by German Fw 190 fighters. *National Archives/Army Air Forces*

This 458th Bomb Group Liberator dubbed *Lassie Come Home* didn't quite make it all the way home on January 14, 1945. Upon returning from a mission to Hallendorf, Germany, the B-24J had one propeller feathered. Nearing Horsham St. Faith, England, the second engine on the same wing quit during a turn, and the pilot lost control. When the plane crashed into a garden in Norwich, England, only one crew member survived. Two children who were playing on the ground also died in the accident. *National Archives/Army Air Forces*

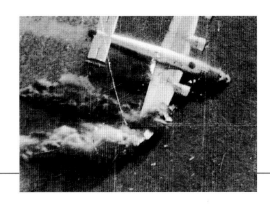

The Bomb Truck

Constantly compared with the B-17, the Consolidated B-24 Liberator was cruelly called "the box that the Flying Fortress came in." But as Liberator crewmen will fervently remind you, there were more Liberators built, and they flew faster, farther, and could carry more bombs than their winged rival. Indeed, the B-24 was more modern than the B-17 and first flew in the last days of 1939.

The bomber incorporated the graceful and marvelously efficient Davis airfoil wing with a chunky, boxcar fuselage and barn-door twin tails. Pilots of this ugly duckling used to say, "It looked like a truck, it hauled like a truck, and it flew like one too." Well loved by those who flew it, the B-24 had its strange traits and difficulties, some of which were downright dangerous.

As with any aircraft design, the B-24 was a compromise. Its modern wing made it fast and efficient—but at a price. Defending the Reich against U.S.

bomber raids, German pilots would often go after the Liberator formations first, if they had the choice. The fighter pilots knew from experience to direct their cannon fire at the wing of a "Flying Boxcar" because it was prone to structural failure and catastrophic fires.

Though blasted and battered, many Liberators managed to withstand serious battle damage and bring their crews back to base. Shot-out engines, gaping holes, and ravaged aircraft components were an all-too-common occurrence in the life-and-death struggles that surrounded a wartime bombing mission. One B-24 even brushed a mountainside one night while trying to locate an airfield in French Morocco. With seven feet of its wing chewed off, the airplane astoundingly flew an additional five times in that condition as the pilot shuttled around Africa, looking for replacement parts. Liberator pilots who had to bring down a damaged craft had to deal with another of the B-24's quirks.

On any other plane besides the Liberator, forced landings were to be made with the wheels up. However, the recommended procedure in the B-24 was to "land with the gear extended on any type of terrain." The reasons were twofold: first, the fuselage of the B-24 was known to crush and break up in belly landings, causing major damage. And second, with the Liberator's high wings, the plane tended to lean to one side after contact with the ground and drag a wingtip. This action often would cause a disastrous wreck, a dangerous fuel fire, or both.

This crew is rarin' to go. The 11-man crew of a Consolidated B-24 Liberator poses for photographers before a mission into Germany. A 10-man crew was most common, but periodically a B-24 would fly with an extra navigator, radio operator, or radar man. *Military History Institute/Dillard Collection*

This image is a testament to the risky business of crash landing a B-24 with the wheels up. On a low-level supply mission in Holland on September 18, 1944, this B-24J of the 491st Bomb Group was hit by flak. Near the town of Udenhout, the stricken Liberator touched down as its starboard wing dug into the soil and broke off. The plane tumbled through the field and into a wooded area. Out of the 10-man crew, only the tail gunner survived the crash. *National Archives/Army Air Forces*

This B-24D of the 30th Bomb Group returned from a bombing mission over Japanese-held territory in the Aleutian Islands only to find its home base on Adak Island fogged in. Choosing nearby Great Sitkin Island for a crash landing, the skillful B-24 pilot made a beautiful belly landing in the soft, waterlogged tundra. Abandoned since January 18, 1943, the remnants of the Liberator reportedly can still be seen in this very spot today. *National Archives/Army Air Forces*

Members of the 353rd Fighter Group work to rescue injured crewmen from the twisted wreckage of a Liberator. In trouble, the B-24's pilots brought the bomber down in the fighter airfield on January 20, 1944. The men appear to be trying to burrow into the cockpit. Note the Plexiglas and metal roof to the pilot's area that is torn away and lying under the crane's boom. A man with an extinguisher stands by on the B-24's port wing in case a fire is sparked during the rescue attempt. *National Archives/Army Air Forces*

A battered B-24J of the 445th Bomb Group is good for nothing but scrap after a collision with a tree lopped off its port wing on March 11, 1944, at Metfield, England. *National Archives/Army Air Forces*

A 307th Bomb Group B-24 with fatal damage plunges toward Negros Island in the Philippines. The bomber was attacked from behind by a Japanese Zero, and observers believed that the fighter was unable to pull out in time to avoid collision. With one vertical fin missing and the starboard wing ripping loose, this Liberator had no chance for survival and crashed into the jungle. *Military History Institute/Milne Collection*

An 88mm antiaircraft shell entered this B-24J of the 449th Bomb Group during a mission over Yugoslavia. The projectile tore through the floor of the plane and didn't explode until striking the ceiling between the waist gunner positions. The blast ripped both .50-caliber guns free of the aircraft, killed one gunner, and severed all the control cables to the tail. The pilot brought the Liberator back home using solely the engines to control pitch and yaw. *National Archives/Army Air Forces*

The crew of a 450th Bomb Group Liberator poses near its battle-ravaged tail. The B-24 rests with its nose wheel off the ground after a mission to Weiner Neustadt, Austria. The plane is believed to have been hit by an attacking enemy fighter with rockets. Some time later in the war, one 450th aircraft pretended to surrender to enemy fighters by lowering its gear, then engaged and shot the opposing aircraft down, and then escaped. After the incident, the distinctive white rudders on the group's planes, nicknamed the Cottontails, were painted over for fear of retribution. *National Archives/Army Air Forces*

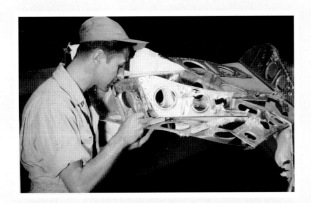

A soldier works to repair the flak-mangled aileron on a Consolidated B-24 Liberator in China.
National Archives/Army Air Forces

Navy Seabees work to quickly move a B-24J named *AWOL* from a runway on Eniwetok Atoll in the Marshall Islands. The starboard main gear failure on this 30th Bomb Group Liberator occurred on April 7, 1944. On another day, this same aircraft suffered a fire in the bomb bay, which disabled the hydraulic system. During that landing, the port main gear folded, leaving poor *AWOL* in a similar position.
National Archives/Navy

Master Sergeant Robert Henman looks over a hole near the tail turret of a Consolidated B-24 in England. The bomber acquired the wound, perhaps inflicted by an enemy fighter, on a mission over Occupied Europe.
National Archives/Army Air Forces

A 504th Bomb Group Superfortress burns as soldiers take cover to avoid exploding ammunition. As the plane returned from a mission to Japan, the brakes of this B-29 locked while it was landing at Iwo Jima on April 24, 1945. The bomber plowed into a row of nine parked P-51 Mustangs before bursting into flames. All members of the crew survived the catastrophic wreck, though two men were burned badly enough to require hospitalization. *National Archives/Army Air Forces*

Pacific Traveler

The long-range Boeing B-29 was ideal for spanning the vast distances of the Pacific Ocean. Bigger and more advanced than the B-24 or B-17, the Superfortress could fly farther, carry more bombs, and go faster than any other bomber in the world. With a modern aerodynamic wing, pressurized and heated crew compartments, and a remote gunnery system, the B-29 represented the pinnacle of World War II aircraft technology.

After problems with engine fires that brought one B-29 prototype down in Seattle during testing, the Superfortress design was improved and readied for combat. Operating from China, B-29s began flying bombing missions in June 1944. But flying from China proved difficult and costly compared to operating from islands in the Pacific, where B-29s could be supplied directly by ship.

By the summer of 1944, the United States had won the islands of Guam, Tinian, and Saipan—about 1,500 miles southeast of Tokyo. The trip to Japan and back took around 15 hours. The first of many B-29 attacks from the Mariana Islands to Japan took place in November 1944.

Superforts stricken by fighters or flak over the target could only look forward to a lonely flight over the seemingly endless Pacific—which was the only real chance for survival. After one raid, a B-29 named *Irish Lassie* limped to Saipan after being rammed twice by Japanese fighters near Tokyo.

On the same day, another Superfortress, *Pride of the Yankees,* made the same long trek with two engines on one wing out of commission.

On March 4, 1945, a B-29 named *Dinah Might* made the first emergency landing on Iwo Jima while a fierce battle still raged for control of the island. A valuable halfway point on the flight path to Japan, Iwo Jima later served as a haven for B-29s that were low on fuel or had been seriously damaged during a mission. The morning after a big raid, the taxiways on Iwo Jima were filled with Superforts that had come in to roost in nearly every condition. They often had transported injured crewman with them.

The possession of Iwo Jima brought another comfort for Superfortress airmen: the addition of fighter protection. Based 750 miles from Japan, P-51 Mustang fighters from Iwo Jima could escort the B-29s on their daytime missions, keeping enemy fighters at bay.

In the last days of the war, specially equipped B-29s dropped two atomic bombs on the Japanese cities of Hiroshima and Nagasaki, hastening Japan's surrender. After World War II, the B-29 continued in service as part of America's Strategic Air Command and fought again in Korea.

The second XB-29 was lost when it crashed into the Frye and Company meat-packing plant in Seattle, Washington, on February 18, 1943. Boeing's flight crew of 11 was killed when the bomber caught fire and plowed into the building three miles north of Boeing Field. Among the dead was famous test pilot Eddie Allen. Nineteen Frye workers and one Seattle fireman were also killed in the "lard-and fat-fueled" blaze that was called the worst in the city's history. *Air Force Historical Research Agency*

Pride of the Yankees of the 500th Bomb Group was attacked by Japanese fighters while hitting the docks in Tokyo on January 27, 1945. The bomber's bullet-riddled No. 2 propeller came completely off the plane, ripping into the turning blades of the No. 1 powerplant. Even with two engines on one wing of the plane destroyed, the crew members of the Pride had little choice but to head out to sea, hoping the plane would last long enough to get them near home. It did more than that: *Pride of the Yankees* made the full retreat of 1,500 miles. It repeated the feat after being similarly damaged in May 1945, making it the only B-29 to twice reach Saipan on two engines. *Bill Agee*

The terrible sacrifices of the marines who fought and died on Iwo Jima began to pay dividends on March 4, 1945. After a mission to the Tokyo area, the 9th Bomb Group's *Dinah Might* arrived on the island low on fuel. As the group's history relates, "The island of Iwo Jima was under terrific bombardment from naval vessels, [and] the marines had just taken the northern airfield. Nevertheless it was the only place to land." As Japanese mortar shells rained down, Dinah retreated to the south end of the airfield to take on fuel and was heading for Tinian within hours. Sadly, *Dinah Might* and her crew were lost during a bombing mission weeks later. *National Archives/Army Air Forces*

Draggin' Lady of the 500th Bomb Group looked as if she would make it back to Isley Field on Saipan until the very last second. The bomber came to rest in the waters right offshore on February 27, 1945. While it looks like these men are enjoying the swim in tropical waters, they are desperately working to rescue the flyers trapped in the forward section of the aircraft. Their efforts were unable to save three men who drowned in *Draggin' Lady*'s nose. *National Archives/Army Air Forces*

This is a view of one of the taxiways on the island of Iwo Jima on the morning after a big raid. The island became a safe haven for bombers with fuel problems, serious battle damage, or wounded crewmen aboard. Here, Tinian's 468th Bomb Group's *L'il Yutz* is parked in the foreground. Other aircraft, with markings representing groups based on Tinian, Guam, and Saipan, can be seen among the tails of the B-29s parked in the background. *National Archives/Army Air Forces*

This was one of the approximately 30 aircraft sent on the first night mission to Tokyo on November 29, 1944. While bombing in the darkness with radar, this B-29 was hit by flak. The nose wheel failed to lower when the bomber returned to Saipan, and the pilot made a textbook two-point landing at Isley Field, causing very little damage to the Superfortress or her crew. Note the smoothly packed runway surface that battered the tips of the B-29's propeller blades. *National Archives/Army Air Forces*

On the night of April 15, 1945, *Ramblin' Roscoe* of the 500th Bomb Group arrived at Iwo Jima with engine and landing gear damage. As the plane touched down on the runway, it hit a truck, killed a Seabee, and injured two men sleeping in a tent before coming to rest on this embankment. In the morning, repair crews looked the plane over to see what could be saved. *National Archives/Army Air Forces*

This was one of a Superfortress flyer's worst nightmares—ditched alone in the vast Pacific Ocean. In this case, the men of this 499th Bomb Group B-29 were very lucky. Discovered by a navy patrol plane 90 miles northwest of Saipan, the men were rescued 17 hours after coming down at sea on December 13, 1944. A destroyer steamed in to pick up the crew, and the B-29, still afloat, was sunk by the ship's guns. *National Archives/Army Air Forces*

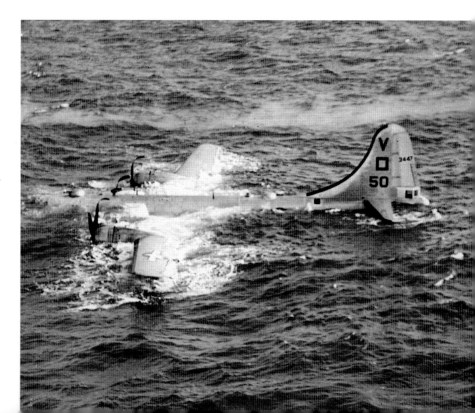

White Mistress of the 6th Bomb Group finds herself in an uncomfortable position off the runway on the island of Tinian. This veteran of more than 40 bombing missions to Japan still carries its defensive armament even though the war has been over for days. B-29s were involved in missions to airdrop supplies to prisoner of war camps throughout Japan, China, Manchuria, and Korea. *The Museum of Flight*

Several bomb groups with aircraft based in the shadow of Mount Vesuvius suffered a sneak attack from nature on March 22, 1944. The historian of the Pompeii-based 340th Bomb Group related the events: "At 8 A.M. all hell broke loose. Black stones of all sizes, some as large as a football, fell in great quantity completely covering the ground, breaking branches from trees, smashing through the tents to break up the floors, tearing through metal, fabric, and plexi-glass [*sic*] of the airplanes." Days later, after escaping the area, members of the group went back to view the damage. "Upon reaching the airport on the 26th," the history continues, "we found almost complete devastation. Tents were torn to ribbons and 88 airplanes were a total loss. Eighty-eight B-25 Mitchells—$25,000,000 worth of aircraft. How Jerry gloated." *National Archives/Army Air Forces*

Billy's Bomber

In the first months of the war, the American public saw photographs of a B-25 bomber, one of Doolittle's Raiders, smashed to bits on a Chinese hilltop after it ran out of fuel and its crew bailed out. Weeks before the war ended, in July 1945, another Mitchell bomber made headlines when it became lost in thick fog and crashed into the 78th and 79th floors of the Empire State Building in New York City. In between, the North American B-25 Mitchell was flown by almost every Allied country and served on every front.

Named for General William "Billy" Mitchell, the B-25 was a fitting tribute to a man who sacrificed his career trying to prove that aircraft could be an invaluable offensive weapon. "Billy's Bombers" proved what he had known all along: slugging it out with the Nazis in North Africa and Europe, sending hundreds of thousands of tons of Japanese shipping to the bottom of the Pacific, and even flying from the deck of an aircraft carrier to attack Tokyo were all missions the B-25 could handle.

The plane's versatility helped keep it in the battle from beginning to end, faithfully conducting bombing missions, low-level attack and strafing, photo-reconnaissance, and transporting VIPs. Some B-25s were still in U.S. Air Force service 20 years after the surrender of Japan.

The Mitchell's sturdy airframe made field modifications and redesign possible, even for those working at the most primitive airfields in the South Pacific. Many "cut and weld jobs" put an arsenal of weapons in the nose of the B-25 in order to mercilessly pound airfields and crack the hulls of enemy vessels like eggshells.

Though it could most certainly "dish it out," the B-25 was popular with airmen because it could also receive a beating and return home. Mitchells touched down safely after direct hits from antiaircraft shells or severe once-overs by enemy fighters. And more than one overanxious flyer came home with the leading edge of his wing pounded in from a collision with a ship's mast on a way-too-low strafing run.

What the Axis couldn't do, sometimes nature could. The 340th Bomb Group had to abandon 88 B-25s during the eruption of Mount Vesuvius in Italy in March 1944. In one of the worst noncombat losses of the war, when the ash finally settled, the singed planes were not much good for anything except spare parts.

Life rafts are placed under the wings of this B-25 damaged in a water landing, to keep it from sinking during salvage efforts in India. It is unclear whether the bomber is being kept afloat in an effort to save the entire plane or simply to strip off desirable parts. Most likely, it was towed ashore to be stripped since it appears that the glass and guns from the top turret have been removed. Either way, the project is not an easy job for Army Air Forces workers assigned to the task. *National Archives/Army Air Forces*

On a high-speed, low-level pass over the Byoritsu oil refinery on Formosa, 498th Bomb Group's *Jaunty Jo* is mortally hit by flak on May 26, 1945. After the strike, the B-25J has a gaping hole in the pilot's side of the cockpit and is beginning to smoke. Seconds after this photo was taken, the bomber tumbled into the ground. The white objects seen off the B-25's starboard wing are parachute-retarded bombs falling over the target. *National Archives/Army Air Forces*

B-25 Mitchells from the 3rd Bomb Group bombed enemy boats in Hansa Bay on August 28, 1943. While piling on the boats, one of the 26 bombers rolled in to deliver its bombs too close behind the preceding aircraft. When one of the boats blew up violently, the explosion engulfed the unlucky Mitchell. *Military History Institute/Bower Collection*

Angel of Mercy, a B-25J from the 310th Bomb Group, was hit by flak and came home with damaged hydraulics. With only the nose wheel deployed, the aircraft was photographed moments after touchdown. With a lot of work done to the engines and nose gear, this bomber was repaired and put back into action. *National Archives/Army Air Forces*

Police and military officials gather around a Mitchell that ran out of runway in Washington, D.C. The slide into this drainage ditch ravaged the plane, leaving close to nothing intact. The removed top turret and faired-over tail gunner position indicate that this plane may have been a ferry plane for stateside military officers rather than a combat-bound bomber. It is also possible that it was one of the B-25s transferred to the Marine Corps and redesignated as a PBJ-1. Many of these patrol bombers were stripped of their turrets late in the war to save weight. *Author's collection*

These radio telephoto news images show the damage caused when a B-25 bomber named *Old John Feather Merchant* crashed into the side of New York's Empire State Building on July 28, 1945. Lost in the fog, the unlucky bomber flew too low and materialized outside the windows of the 78th and 79th floors—975 feet over Fifth Avenue. Thirteen people, including the airplane's three-man crew, were killed in the accident. The image below shows a hole in the roof of a nearby studio in the 12-story Waldorf Building, which was ripped open by falling debris. *Author's collection*

A B-25 Mitchell of the 12th Bomb Group lies in a marshy area near the runway at Fenny, India. Flyers in the area came to know the plane as the *Swamp Queen*. These two men couldn't help but take advantage of a photo opportunity posed in the derelict bomber's well-ventilated cockpit. *Hank Redmond via Stan Piet*

This B-26C, *Junior*, of the 391st Bomb Group encountered an 88mm antiaircraft shell on a mission to Beaumont-sur-Oise, France, on May 20, 1944. With its tail an amazing mess of junk, the plane made it home to be ogled by a shocked and unbelieving ground crew. *National Archives/Army Air Forces*

B Dash-Crash

The Martin B-26 lived and died amid controversy. The streamlined, high-speed, and innovative bomber was almost too much for all but the best pilots and mechanics to handle when it appeared in 1940, leading to stateside accidents and mistrust among army flyers. When some of the earliest B-26 bombing missions ended in disaster, the losses did nothing to quell the malicious rumors among soldiers, politicians, and the public that the airplane was a deathtrap.

The B-26 was officially called the Marauder, but air crews found other names. A fast bomber with a small wing area, it was disparagingly called "The Flying Vagrant," "The Wingless Wonder," or "The Baltimore Whore." Other distrusting souls dubbed the B-26 "The Coffin Without Handles," "The Widow Maker," and "B Dash-Crash."

Over time, however, army commanders and B-26 crewmen learned how to exploit the B-26's good traits, leaving the gloom and doom far behind the speedy bomber. A prolonged combat role for the B-26 in the Pacific was ruled out. B-25s could take off in less space, had more propeller clearance, and were much easier to maintain—all ideal for primitive island operations. Low-level attack-type missions also were scrubbed. The Marauder was a medium bomber that would do its best work at medium altitudes while carrying a Norden bombsight. As crews spent more time handling the B-26, performance improved and accidents became less frequent.

The Marauder shined in the European Theater. Crewmen found the plane tough, its sturdy airframe able to absorb hits from antiaircraft fire and bring them back over the English Channel. Marauders were effective at hitting comparatively small targets, such as German V-1 launch sites, rail yards, and airfields, and assisting army ground forces by bombing troublesome concentrations of enemy troops and equipment. By war's end, the B-26 had dropped 150,000 tons of bombs and achieved the lowest loss rate of any Allied bomber—less than one-half of one percent per sortie.

When the Germans surrendered in May 1945, the Marauder's bad reputation seemed to catch up with the bomber once again. Rather than making the long but victorious flight back to the United States, most Marauders were blown up, bulldozed, and carted away to smelters, supplying scrap metal for Germany's new postwar industries. Their glory days behind them, surviving B-26s were soon stricken from the U.S. Army's inventory—the Douglas A-26 Invader was redesignated B-26.

This interesting shot of crewmen inside a Martin B-26C Marauder was taken by Captain Joseph Merhar Jr., commander of the 9th Air Division Photo Laboratory in England. *Air Force Historical Research Agency*

After hitting the Roccasecca Bridge in Italy, a B-26C of the 17th Bomb Group named *Uden Uden's Oil Burner* struggles to stay near the protective guns of the other aircraft in its formation. The bomber was hit by antiaircraft fire that knocked out its port engine. The pilot feathered the propeller and ordered the crew to lighten the load. This photograph shows a belt of .50-caliber ammunition being tossed from a gun port of the injured Marauder. *Military History Institute/Milne Collection*

This 323rd Bomb Group B-26 named *Circle Jerk* was hit on a mission to Eller Bridge in Germany. In this image, taken southeast of the target near Wittlich, the torque from the plane's still-running starboard engine rolls the plane on its back as the entire port engine, complete with cowling, plummets away. The bomber was one of two aircraft that the 323rd lost on December 23, 1944. *National Archives/Army Air Forces*

After an attack on Lanuvio, Italy, on February 17, 1944, this 320th Bomb Group bomber didn't make it home to the island of Sardinia. After it was reported that "Aircraft No. 79 is missing and was last seen over Nettuno," the plane tried a landing at Nettuno Airfield, and this was the result. Amazingly, all the men on board the B-26 survived what must have been a spectacular accident. *National Archives/Army Air Forces*

A 323rd Bomb Group B-26G tangled with a "cletrac" on takeoff on December 23, 1944. Called the cletrac by flyers, and used for towing and lifting aircraft and vehicles, the M2 tractor was built by the Cleveland Tractor Company and was a standard fixture at many airfields in England. Here, an out-of-control Marauder has upended one of the 13,000-pound machines as if it was a toy, causing heavy damage to both the vehicle and the aircraft. *National Archives/Army Air Forces*

With its olive green skin spattered by shrapnel, this B-26B nicknamed *Earthquake McGoon* from the 17th Bomb Group flies toward its home at Telergma, Algeria, on March 24, 1943. Note the crewman peeking at the damage through the Plexiglas astrodome seen over the bomber's mangled port wing. Without a doubt, the flyers in the adjoining plane were amazed at what they saw. Martin Aircraft used this image (with the plane's serial number airbrushed out) in one of its ads, commenting, "Four-hundred thousand rivets hold Martin Marauders together even when shot up like this one flying home over Tunisia." *National Archives/Army Air Forces*

This B-26 crash is not what it seems. The worn-out or damaged Marauder is being used to train ground crews in handling accidents and injured aircrew at the Army Air Forces Service Group Training Center in Greenville, South Carolina. *Military History Institute/Milne Collection*

A sorry sight for those who flew the B-26 into battle, a former 344th Bomb Group plane named *Heaven Can Wait* is blown to bits at Landsberg, Germany, after VE-Day. The veteran of 99 bombing raids is turned from a $200,000 fighting machine to a pile of scrap with 20 pounds of TNT. The shattered pieces were gathered and trucked away to German smelters. *National Archives/Army Air Forces*

Shopworn Angel of the 344th Bomb Group lies with both of its propellers chewed up and one main gear collapsed. The pilot of the B-26B on this mission was Captain Lucius B. Clay, son of the famous general who would later organize the Berlin Airlift. The date of the photograph is unknown. *Jack Havener via Stan Piet*

Fire has consumed this late-model A-20 in Iceland on May 16, 1944. It appears that the aircraft burned on the ground rather than being involved in a crash. Visible in the photo is Aero Foam, a flame retardant that some airmen called bean soup. Veterans recall that the foam concoction contained animal blood protein; other versions were made from soybean protein and water. *National Archives/Army Air Forces*

On the Attack

Early French and British versions of the Douglas A-20, called the DB-7 Boston, were fighting the Nazis even before the United States entered World War II. On the Fourth of July, 1942, six American army crews joined six British crews in the Douglas bombers for a raid on Dutch airfields—the war's first daylight U.S. bombing mission in Europe. The famous aircraft saw action worldwide in Europe, North Africa, the Pacific, and even on the Eastern Front with Russian forces.

Like many successful aircraft of the era, the A-20 was adapted to perform a large number of different tasks. Besides having the ability to conduct bombing missions and low-level attacks, the aircraft was outfitted as a radar-equipped night fighter and high-speed photo-reconnaissance platform. The British even created a version of the Douglas aircraft that carried a 2.7-billion-candlepower searchlight in its nose, called a Tubinlite.

Many A-20s in the Pacific were modified into gunships and strafers by installing machine guns in the bombardier's compartment in the nose and using parachute-retarded bombs that could be dropped at treetop or wave-top level. Not all the changes to these attack planes were offensive in nature—steel armor plates often were placed under the flyers' seats.

By late 1944, the army had another Douglas attack aircraft in its inventory. The A-26 Invader was faster, bigger, and heavier than its older brother and saw immediate success in the skies over Europe. A problem of a weak nose-gear strut that collapsed during early operations was easily overcome with modifications, and an improved canopy eased complaints about pilot visibility over the large R-2800 engines.

On rare occasions, the crews of the big A-26s even tangled with enemy fighters, holding their own, shooting it out with nose-mounted machine guns, and sometimes even claiming victories. But most combat damage came in the form of heavy flak, with A-26s limping home from a target with a dead engine or a collection of holes punched through the fuselage and wings.

Because of its long nose and high-placed engines, the A-26 was not as well suited for low-level attacks as was the A-20. But the Invader did see action in the Pacific, hitting targets in Okinawa, Formosa, China, and the home islands of Japan before the surrender. After the war, Invaders continued to serve with the U.S. Air Force through the Korean War and into Vietnam.

Showing off a bit of its handiwork, a 410th Bomb Group Douglas A-20G Havoc named *Queen Julias* cruises over a bomb-pitted enemy airfield. *National Archives/Army Air Forces*

A dip in the runway at the Second Base Air Depot in Lancashire, England, claimed three airplanes on one day—October 5, 1944. First, a 466th Bomb Group Liberator slid off the runway on landing. Next, this A-20K hit the same dip while returning from a test flight, swerved to avoid the injured B-24 (seen in the background), and slid to a stop with collapsed gear and its nose pounded in. And, to add insult to injury, a new P-51D Mustang came in later that day and cracked up while trying to avoid hitting the other two stranded aircraft. *National Archives/Army Air Forces*

Straddling the line between sea and land, this army bomber went down near a navy airfield on October 8, 1942. The feathered propeller on the port side makes one believe the A-20A was having engine problems before skidding to a stop near the runways of the U.S. Naval Air Station at Argentia in Newfoundland, Canada. No one was injured among the airplane's crewmen. *National Archives/Navy*

As two A-20s from the 312th Bomb Group race away from Japanese targets at Kokas, New Guinea, one of the raiders is mortally wounded by antiaircraft fire. Twelve aircraft carrying 48 250-pound bombs hit the heavily defended installation on July 22, 1944. Here, First Lieutenant James Knarr's A-20G is caught in the intense gunfire over the target and plunges into the water nearby. *Shu Shu Baby*, the plane from which these pictures were taken, returned home with more than 100 bullet and shell holes. *National Archives/Army Air Forces*

On March 1, 1943, this A-20B chose the sand flats near the U.S. Naval Air Station at Guantanamo Bay, Cuba, for a belly landing. It is unknown what caused this trouble in paradise, but the undamaged condition of the attack bomber's propellers leads one to suspect that the propellers were turning slowly, or not at all, at the time of the impact. Navy men, Cuban workers, and, perhaps, some of the A-20's crew quickly break out the toolboxes and begin to cart away desirable equipment from the wreck. *National Archives/Navy*

On August 26, 1944, 33 aircraft of the 386th Bomb Group attacked a target at Bois-de-Mont, France. The very short entry in the unit's history says, "All aircraft returned safely." This muddy and mangled A-26 photographed at the 386th's home in Great Dunmow, England, that day makes one wonder how safe the mission really was. It is unknown how or where this aircraft sustained such damage. *National Archives/Army Air Forces*

With one propeller blade jammed straight into the ground, this Invader's starboard main landing gear appears to have given way as it stood parked at Beaumont-sur-Oise, France, on April 10, 1945. The 386th Bomb Group aircraft shows evidence of a "nose job." Though it was not uncommon for solid and Plexiglas noses to be changed out, records show that this A-26C was delivered from Douglas' Tulsa, Oklahoma, plant with a transparent nose. Perhaps the plane had been repaired after it suffered a nose-gear failure on a previous flight. *National Archives/Army Air Forces*

Chapter 3

Fighters

On December 20, 1944, this 8th Fighter Group P-38L was badly shot up in an air battle with Japanese fighters over Mindoro Island in the Philippines. With his port engine throwing coolant and his main gas tank hit, Second Lieutenant Francis Ford stayed in the fight, gathering more holes in his aircraft. When his port engine conked out, Ford brought his Lightning down. Though it almost immediately burst into flames upon landing, Ford was able to escape from the crashed fighter unharmed.
Military History Institute/Milne Collection

Fork-Tailed Devil

The army decided to use its sleek new prototype P-38 Lightning fighter in an attempt to break the transcontinental speed record in early 1939. From California to New York, everything went as planned until the last seconds of the flight, when the plane crash-landed onto a golf course just short of the runway. The pilot, Lieutenant Ben Kelsey, was unhurt in the crash and joked, "There is nothing wrong with the ship. It was just that damn fool pilot." It was no matter; the plane was a winner, setting a new record and being touted as the army's first 400-mile-per-hour fighter.

The Lockheed Lightning was an unusual aircraft. Its tricycle landing gear, twin engines, and unique twin tail separated it from any other U.S. fighter that had been built before. In the early days of the war, it was the P-38 (along with the often-outclassed P-39 and P-40) that formed the backbone of the army's fighter force. The radical design of the Lightning gave it many pleasing characteristics, including no torque from the counter-rotating propellers, concentrated armament in its nose, and extraordinary range and power.

The Lightning's two-engine arrangement was a sort of give-and-take proposition. One P-38 came home safely on one engine after striking a telephone pole. Another smashed almost headlong into a German Bf 109 and also returned with a single engine operating. These pilots and many others most likely owed their lives to the twin-powerplant Lightning. But the advantage of two engines could also prove deadly for the inexperienced pilot. Engine malfunction always was a problem with the plane, and a failure on landing or takeoff led to many accidents as the surprised pilot struggled to manage the unbalanced thrust. It became a well-known rumor that a P-38 pilot coming in on a single engine was "one sad sack."

Lockheed publications countered: "It isn't hard to fly on one engine—it's just knowing how."

Another nagging concern always in the back of a Lightning pilot's head was, if the time came, how the plane could be left safely. The bladelike horizontal stabilizer between the double booms looked like a guillotine, poised to swipe at an escaping flyer. Lockheed recommended that pilots crawl out and slide off the wing headfirst. Airmen weren't so sure.

Even after fighters like the P-47 and P-51 took over fighter duties in Europe, the P-38 continued to excel in the Pacific. America's top two aces of all time, Richard Bong and Thomas McGuire, accounted for shooting down 78 Japanese aircraft combined, all while flying the Lightning.

A flight of Fifteenth Air Force Lockheed P-38L Lightning fighters prowls the skies over Italy in 1944. *National Archives/Army Air Forces*

At the end of a successful cross-country dash on February 11, 1939, the U.S. Army's prototype XP-38 came down at Cold Stream Golf Course just short of Mitchell Field, New York. As the tower asked pilot Ben Kelsey to come in to land behind some slower-moving fighters, he throttled back to about 15 percent power and dropped his flaps and gear. When it came time to add more power, the engines did not respond, perhaps due to icing of the carburetors. The XP-38 hit some trees and then flopped to the ground. *Corbis*

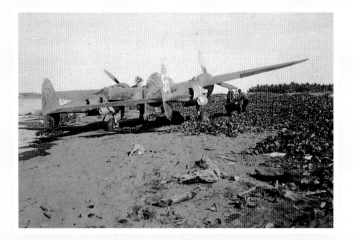

On January 21, 1943, the 1st Fighter Group participated in an attack near Tripoli, Libya. While diving down to the deck to shoot at German trucks, this Lightning, flown by Lieutenant Benton Miller, struck a telephone pole. Even with one propeller missing, a horribly twisted wing, and crushed gun bay door acting as a speed brake, Miller amazingly was able to keep the P-38F above stall speed and limp back to Biskra, Algeria, for a perfect landing. *Kenneth Sumney*

They say any landing that you can walk away from is a good one. This landing, considering the circumstances, was nothing short of excellent. Brought down "somewhere in the Pacific" in the soft sand, this P-38 looks none the worse for wear. "Now," the ground crewmen say, "how in the heck are we going to get this heavy bird out of here?" *Military History Institute/Varga Collection*

Lieutenant Fred Erbele of the 318th Fighter Group tangled with Japanese antiaircraft defenses on Iwo Jima on January 5, 1945. Pulling off the target, the port engine of his P-38L quit and his starboard wing burst into flames. When it began to look as if he'd have no choice but to bail out, Erbele jettisoned the top panel of his canopy, but soon after, the fire died away, revealing a large hole. For four hours and 40 minutes, the flyer coaxed the wounded Lightning back to Saipan, while being shadowed by a pair of B-24s. This image, snapped from one of the bombers, shows the damage inflicted on the craft, including the unfeathered and immobile port propeller, blown-off spinner, and the large hole in the starboard wing. *National Archives/Army Air Forces*

In a sight that breaks the heart of any World War II aviation enthusiast, these 343rd Fighter Group P-38Ls are left as scrap for salvage on Shemya Island in the Aleutians. This late in the war, these planes were most likely lost due to weather-related accidents. Rumor has it that when the war was over, these planes were either buried on the island or dumped into the sea. *National Archives/Army Air Forces*

There is little doubt that when this P-38G hit, it hit hard. During transition training at Wright Field in Ohio on July 14, 1943, the nose gear in this Lightning collapsed during what the accident report calls "a terrifically hard landing." The propellers flew from the aircraft, and the startled and stunned pilot quickly escaped the cockpit while the engines were still roaring. "For the safety of personnel," the report continued, "it was necessary to remain clear of the wreckage until the engines had stopped by 'freezing.'" *Air Force Historical Research Agency*

A Lockheed F-5, a photo-reconnaissance version of the Lightning, from the 6th Photo Reconnaissance Group was on a mission to photograph the airfields at Hollandia, New Guinea, when it developed engine trouble. Coming in on one motor at Tadji, Lieutenant Hewitt Clark overshot the runway, hit a Curtiss P-40, and skidded into a swampy area near the end of the airstrip. An Australian mechanic was killed in the accident, the aircraft was lost, and Clark suffered a broken leg. These photos show the plane after the April 30, 1944, accident and the ground crew treating the dazed pilot. *Military History Institute/Milne Collection*

The pilot of this 18th Fighter Group P-38 Lightning named *Rickie Boy* pulls in close to his wingman somewhere over the Pacific. While many army pilots considered flying the Lightning with only one engine tricky, it saved plenty of lives. *The Museum of Flight/Army Air Forces*

An 80th Fighter Group Curtiss P-40N Warhawk carries a special message for Tojo on a bomb slung under its belly. The photo was taken at Nagaghuli Air Base in Upper Assam, India, in February 1944. *National Archives/Army Air Forces*

Second Class in First String

In the early days of America's involvement in the war, the country called upon the Bell P-39 and Curtiss P-40 to defend its interests all over the globe. Mixing it up with the superior fighters and combat-experienced pilots of the Axis air forces, unlucky army pilots often found that they couldn't out-dive, out-climb, or outmaneuver fighters like the Zero or Bf 109. In these early skirmishes, one dreary reality was learned the hard way: American-made fighter planes could generally take a lot of punishment.

The P-39 Airacobra flew first, in April 1938. The plane featured a radical design, with its engine-mounted amidships and a 37mm cannon built into its nose. Many army flyers were suspicious of the layout, insisting that a mid-engine plane "wouldn't know what way is down" when it went into a spin. The slanderous mess song they created says it all:

Don't give me a P-39,
With an engine that's mounted behind,
It will tumble and roll,
And dig a big hole,
Don't give me a P-39.

When the Curtiss P-40 first flew in October 1939, it carried the same basic Allison engine as the P-39, but up in its nose. Though it was called a "pilot's plane" by those who flew it, the P-40 was behind the times when it was introduced and never really seemed to catch up. The Curtiss fighter was important in early fighting because it was available and could be built quickly. As a result of that, it served with almost all Allied countries.

Deemed "inferior" by German pilots interviewed after the war, both the Bell P-39 and Curtiss P-40 went out of production before hostilities ceased. Other American fighters, like the P-51 and P-47, took over as the workhorses of the army's fighter force.

Another aircraft added to the U.S. Army's fighter fleet was the British Supermarine Spitfire. Under reverse lend-lease agreements, about 1,000 Spitfires made it into American squadrons, first with the Eighth Air Force in England and later with the Twelfth Air Force in North Africa and Italy. American pilots took time getting used to the Spit's strange-feeling weight distribution and the "foreign" braking system. Embarrassingly, a number of these beautiful machines ended up crumpled or crashed during the first few months of service, while their new owners learned the ropes.

An Italian news photograph shows two P-40Fs (perhaps of the 325th Fighter Group) caught by falling bombs where they were parked on the Tunisian front. Note the 48-star American flag decals affixed to the lower surfaces of the port wings. The starboard wings carried the more-familiar white and blue star insignia. *Author's collection*

This 23rd Fighter Group P-40N was innocently parked on the fighter strip at Kweilin, China, when it ran into trouble. The pilot of a P-51 ran its wingtip into the parked Warhawk on takeoff. Upon reviewing the damage, crewmen joked that it looked like the shark-faced P-40 had taken a bite out of its faster and more modern comrade. The P-40 was that of ace Donald Lopez. The cowling was quickly repaired, but it took a little longer for crewmen to paint the mouth back on the plane. Lopez mentioned in his autobiography that he ". . . became a toothless tiger and had to gum the Japs for several weeks." *National Archives/Army Air Forces*

The canvas cover worn by this injured P-40 in Iceland is pulled back to access the cockpit as crewmen begin to assess the damage caused by a main gear failure on March 15, 1944. After a few days' work in these less-than-perfect conditions, this Warhawk will be in the air again. *National Archives/Army Air Forces*

This Bell P-39D went down in an unknown location in the United States on October 24, 1942. This Airacobra may well have "tumbled and rolled," yet it didn't "dig a big hole" as the old song claimed it would. Note that the heavy engine, located in the middle of the plane, sunk deeper into the ground upon impact than the shattered cockpit. *National Archives/Army Air Forces*

Another P-39D is seen laid out on the hard soil of a farmer's field near Piqua, Ohio, on April 26, 1943. Investigation indicated that a runaway propeller was the initial cause of the accident. Witnesses saw the plane enter into a flat spin at 2,000 feet, and investigators reported that "the aircraft struck the ground flat with very low speed. Examination of the propeller indicates that it was not turning at the time of impact, indicating that forward speed was too low for the propeller to windmill." *Air Force Historical Research Agency*

This P-39Q was being ferried to Russia when it ran into trouble on the runway in Nome, Alaska. During what would have been its last landing in U.S. territory, the nose gear collapsed and the main gears partially folded. The Airacobra rests with fuel slowly leaking from its large belly tank, while crewmen figure how to best save the ship. Note that the P-39's unique automobile-style cockpit door swung open on the fighter's starboard side. *National Archives/Army Air Forces*

A Sicily-based Spitfire Mk V of the American 31st Fighter Group lies just offshore during the invasion of Italy at the Gulf of Salerno in early September 1943. While covering the invasion beaches, the plane was shot down by antiaircraft guns near Paestum. The veteran aircraft shows victory markings—three small swastikas—on the fuselage under the canopy. *Peter Bowers Collection*

This flak-damaged 52nd Fighter Group Spitfire Mk VC has seen its last combat as soldiers strip it down to nothing on February 13, 1943, in North Africa. Using the port wing of the aircraft as their workbench, they are carefully laying out pieces of the fighter's guts, which are destined for transplants into other fighters. Note that before getting elbow-deep in Spitfire parts, one of the men has hung his leather jacket out of the way on the doomed plane's radio mast. *National Archives/Army Air Forces*

This 31st Fighter Group Spitfire MK V was involved in a wreck near Membury, England, while American pilots trained on the fighter in 1942. In the caption that accompanies the photo in its album, an airman has written, almost apologetically, "Our pilots could not get used to the brakes." Another member of the 31st wrote this in his diary on July 14, 1942: "Officers meeting in the morning. In the past 16 days, 21 planes have been destroyed or badly damaged, most of them by 308 Squadron. That's too many, and due to carelessness, says Colonel Hawkins."
The Museum of Flight/Dyche Collection

Rows of worn Curtiss P-40s stand upended in Walnut Ridge, Arkansas, awaiting final destruction. The fighters have been stripped of their engines and are stacked in compact rows to take up minimal space. The aircraft in the foreground is a P-40 N-model Warhawk. *National Archives/Army Air Forces*

This P-47D of the Ninth Air Force came back from a mission with a hung-up 500-pound bomb under one wing. A bounce on landing jolted the bomb loose, with these catastrophic results, on January 1, 1945. Amazingly, the pilot of this rolling wreck was only slightly injured in the blast. *National Archives/Army Air Forces*

Seven-Ton Milk Jug

Stories of the Republic P-47 Thunderbolt and its toughness are told with great enthusiasm by the men who flew the plane in combat. One P-47 pilot says that while strafing a truck, he kept his guns firing too long, pulled up too late, and flew *through* the vehicle. Scores of others sheepishly stepped down from their aircraft after an attack mission and began to pick tree parts from their crushed cowlings and wings. "I hit a bird" was the common excuse. Not fooled, the squadron commander might observe, "It looks like you hit him while he was sitting in a tree."

The fighter named Thunderbolt hardly was ever called as such by those who took the plane aloft. To them, it was "The Flying Bulldozer," "The Iron Monster," or "Bag O' Bolts." Some flyers claim that the P-47's most famous nickname, "Jug," is short for "Juggernaut." Others say that the name came from the shape of the plane's fuselage, which became especially noticeable when it nosed over during a rough landing. The plane reminded observers of these accidents of a milk jug—"a Seven-ton Milk Jug."

First flown in May 1941, the P-47 was the biggest and heaviest single-engine fighter to reach production during World War II. The combination of a hearty airframe and a big air-cooled engine made the Jug able to sustain horrible damage and return its pilot to safety. German pilots observed that a P-47 could absorb direct hits from their cannon-equipped fighters and continue to fly and fight. The Jug's R-2800 engine often would keep running even after a cylinder had been shot away or had virtually no oil left inside.

Made for high-altitude operation, the Thunderbolt had sturdy traits that made it ideal for the role of ground attack as well. Particularly after D-Day,

German tanks, trains, troops, and trucks were hounded and hunted by P-47s that swarmed the countryside, looking for something to pound with their bombs and eight machine guns.

The Jug was loved by airmen, who felt that the plane would protect them at all costs. One pilot got teased by his buddies after his P-47 was hit and heavily damaged and he refused to bail out. Even when a fire sprang to life under the cowling and he was ordered to leave, the flyer stubbornly stayed with his machine and managed to crash-land on the friendly side of the front lines. It just seemed like a safer bet to stick with a Thunderbolt—even a dying Thunderbolt—than to take the chance of bailing out over enemy-held territory.

Shiny new Republic P-47N Thunderbolts cruise over the Pacific late in the war. The N-model was designed to escort B-29s over Japan, with a range of more than 2,000 miles. *The Museum of Flight*

A German truck loaded with ammunition or fuel creates a spectacular explosion under the machine-gun fire of a Ninth Air Force P-47, throwing fire and pieces of debris into the air in all directions. This famous photo, captured by the wingman's gun camera, shows one of the common dangers of ground-attack missions. The Thunderbolt that was caught in the blast is reported to have made it home safely. *National Archives/Army Air Forces*

On April 1, 1945, Lieutenant Richard Sulzbach of the 350th Fighter Group was harassing German trucks while flying his Thunderbolt, *Buzzin' Cousin*. After missing his target once, his squadron's history relates the rest of the story: "Getting peeved he decided to really get them on the second pass—he did but as he swooped low towards the trucks, a few treetops got in his way. His sturdy Thunderbolt pulled up and away from the treetops and he began to nurse the crippled sky bird back to base." Upon seeing the damage, "the small, cocky pilot [seen on the left in this photograph] did not have the usual grin on his face, all he could say was, 'If I would have realized that boat was in that bad of shape I do not believe I would have brought her home.' " *National Archives/Army Air Forces*

Pilots joked that the P-47 ran best when most of the oil stayed inside the engine. Lieutenant Edwin King of the 350th Fighter Group came home to Pisa, Italy, the hard way and found that a Jug can go, for at least a short time, with hardly any oil at all. An oil line in his P-47D was hit during a strafing mission near Brizsua, Italy, on the plane's 110th combat mission. King most probably attempted his hair-raising, no forward visibility landing by flying in formation with a wingman. *National Archives/Army Air Forces*

A P-47D of the 353rd Fighter Group lies on its belly at Raydon, England, on August 13, 1944. *Smoocher* will require a bit of work but will fly once more. Note the bent barrel of the damaged innermost .50-caliber machine gun on the port wing. *National Archives/Army Air Forces*

Investigators believe this 353rd Fighter Group P-47D was running perfectly when it slammed into an English country house on September 5, 1943. The Eighth Air Force blamed personnel for 90 percent of the accident. The report of the accident noted that ". . . the pilot, who was killed, failed to check weather thoroughly but informed the flying control officer that he had." The other 10 percent was blamed on weather, which forced the Thunderbolt pilot to drop too low in heavy cloud cover. *National Archives/Army Air Forces*

All this pilot could do was stare in amazement at the freakish hit through the propeller blade of his P-47D. If it had been damaged a fraction of an inch in either direction, the whirling blade would have no doubt come apart and brought the big fighter down. Edwin Wright was the 19-year-old pilot. Many pilots said that by the time you reached the age of 25, "old man status," you were much too wise to fly attack missions in a Thunderbolt. *National Archives/Army Air Forces*

This P-47D of the 365th Fighter Group went down along the Normandy coast from antiaircraft damage during support of D-Day operations. The pilot picked a nice place to bring his injured bird in for an emergency landing and probably escaped injury. In this photo, a curious GI has a look into the long-gone flyer's "office" inside the downed fighter on July 2, 1944. *The Museum of Flight/Army Air Forces*

This P-51D named *Frances A.* of the 364th Fighter Group had its tail shredded on December 8, 1944. The damage most likely came as the aircraft was parked and struck by another moving Mustang. Note the shattered Plexiglas canopy on the mangled fighter. *National Archives/Army Air Forces*

Cadillac of the Skies

The P-51 Mustang was arguably the best fighter of World War II. Mustang pilots slyly said that everything a Spitfire could do in 20 minutes, the Mustang could do all day. The Mustang's ability to fly long distances made it a great escort for protecting heavy bombers on missions into Occupied Europe and Germany. And when their fuel finally got low, P-51 pilots went down on the deck and turned toward home, eagerly blasting anything of value that was unlucky enough to cross their path.

The Mustang was born when the British approached North American Aviation about building P-40s under license for the Royal Air Force (RAF). The California-based company designed and built an entirely new and better Allison-powered airplane in an amazing 117 days. After only five flights, the prototype was involved in a wreck, but the British were sold, and the orders kept coming. When it came time to name the new fighter, perhaps someone in the British Air Council recalled the 1936 tune that went, "Saddle your blues to a mustang and gallop your troubles away, away." The name "Mustang" sounded wild and American. It had a cowboy feel to it.

After it was mated with a Rolls-Royce Merlin engine, the P-51 airframe found even greater success with the U.S. Army Air Forces, which ordered more than 14,800 of all types. Serving in nearly every combat zone, the Mustang excelled as a bomber escort, a role in which, flying with two 108-gallon drop tanks, the fighter could stay in the air for seven or eight hours.

But one of the P-51's greatest traits—its extreme range—also could get a pilot into a whole mess of trouble. Miles and miles away from the nearest friendly airfield, pilots always had that nagging feeling that one lucky shot into a Mustang's liquid-coolant system could turn his dreamy flying machine into a gliding hunk of junk in a matter of minutes—or even seconds.

Famed German fighter pilot Adolf Galland and others interviewed after the war told U.S. interrogators that the Mustang was "the best American fighter," but added, "It was very vulnerable to cannon fire." Luftwaffe pilots also mentioned that they had seen P-51s break up during very violent dives and maneuvers.

After the war, another statement about the famed fighter surfaced during the questioning of Reichsmarschall Hermann Göring, head of the Luftwaffe. He said, "When I saw Mustangs over Berlin, I knew the war was lost."

A drop tank–equipped North American P-51D Mustang of the 361st Fighter Group named *Sky Bouncer* shows off in the "footless halls of air" over Europe. *National Archives/Army Air Forces*

On the Mustang prototype's fifth flight, the Allison engine quit on test pilot Paul Balfour while attempting a landing at Mines Field, California, on November 20, 1940. The fighter came down in a field, with its landing gear extended, and promptly flipped over on its back. Balfour had to wait while rescuers dug a hole for him to escape near the overturned plane's canopy. In this image, note the shovel near the port wing of the shiny new fighter. *The Boeing Company Archives*

A P-51D Mustang named *Jackie* from the 364th Fighter Group stalled out on takeoff and plowed into the tail of a parked B-17 in Honnington, England, on July 30, 1944. In the wreck and ensuing fire, two ground crewmen were injured and the fighter pilot killed. In the image to the right, men remove the body of First Lieutenant James Korecky from the badly burned wreckage. *National Archives/Army Air Forces*

Like an army of carpenter ants, workmen swarm all over this 364th Fighter Group Mustang named *Lady Eleanor*. The fighter bellied in at Honnington, England, on April 25, 1945. The canopy, if it was still in good shape, was always one of the first things to be salvaged. Also, for safety reasons, the ammunition from the fighter's .50-caliber machine guns was quickly removed. *National Archives/Army Air Forces*

The pilot of this 506th Fighter Group P-51D was a lucky man on May 28, 1945. Fully loaded with fuel for a mission to Japan, the plane slid off a runway at Iwo Jima on takeoff. The careening fighter shed its drop tanks and fuel-filled wings along the island's rocky landscape, where both the tanks and wings immediately burst into flames. The fuselage came to rest with its tail in the blaze and its canopy jammed. The pilot no doubt endured some of the longest minutes of his life as he waited for help to arrive and free him from the wreckage. The flyer walked away (or more realistically ran away) from the crash with no injuries. *National Archives/Army Air Forces*

As other Mustangs take to the skies, this 353rd Fighter Group P-51D named *Danny Boy 2nd* lies on the frozen grass at Raydon, England. A ground loop takeoff terminated the mission before it had even begun for Captain Melvin Hightshoe and his Mustang on December 29, 1944. His first aircraft, named simply *Danny Boy*, was lost in combat a month earlier with another pilot at the controls. *National Archives/Army Air Forces*

The crane hangs overhead like a hangman's noose, waiting to take away what remains of this 353rd Fighter Group Mustang on September 4, 1944. With almost every useable panel, piece, or part taken off and carted away, this skeleton is on its way to becoming scrap metal for Britain's war industry. It is possible to imagine that the raw material from this Mustang was used to make parts of a later-model Spitfire fighter. *National Archives/Army Air Forces*

Amid a lake of fire-fighting foam at Honnington, England, this P-51D of the 364th Fighter Group rests on its belly. When the spinning propeller from an aircraft hit the ground, it usually totally destroyed the engine. Note the fighter's fire-singed front windscreen and rearview mirror. *National Archives/Army Air Forces*

Famous ace Don Gentile of the 4th Fighter Group finished his final combat mission on April 13, 1944. Upon returning from Schweinfurt, Germany, he decided to give the boys at Debden, England, a show. While the soldiers and press looked on, Gentile flew too low on one of his high-speed passes and his plane's propeller touched the ground. He belly-landed his P-51, named *Shangri-La*, into a nearby field. The man that President Roosevelt had once called "captain courageous" was unhurt in the accident. The army promptly released photos of the plane but didn't tell the real story behind the damage. *Shangri-La*'s death was called a combat casualty—not the result of what airmen termed "flathatting." *The Museum of Flight/Army Air Forces*

A Japanese bomb cleanly sliced the nose off this C-47 at Kweilin, China. What appears to be the pilot's seat and the cockpit bulkhead can be seen in the jumbled mass of the fuselage. Though the rest of the plane has suffered very little damage, it is doubtful that personnel will have enough time and parts to get the plane flying again. *National Archives/Army Air Forces*

Doing It All

Like an unseen stagehand in a massive theatrical production, cargo aircraft in all theaters of the war covered millions of miles while thanklessly lugging the ammunition, bombs, spare parts, and fuel used to keep a massive air force on the move "from one godforsaken place to the next." Though often spared from combat, the men who crewed the "Gooney Birds" and "Dumbos" nevertheless encountered more than their fair share of danger. The routes were rough, the hours were long, and the surroundings were often deadly.

As the specter of war loomed over Europe and the Pacific, the U.S. Army concentrated on amassing its bomber forces, leaving the subject of a cargo and transport fleet neglected. When war came, the army and navy adopted many civilian transport designs, while airliners that already had been produced were pressed into war service.

The 1936 Douglas DC-3 passenger plane became the army's workhorse—the C-47. The "Gooney Bird," as it was lovingly called by the GIs, moved troops and toted cargo to every corner of the globe. During airborne assaults, including D-Day, C-47s towed gliders and dropped paratroopers amid hellish antiaircraft fire. Flyers loved the Douglas craft because it was strong, reliable, and tough. An army C-47 pilot's training manual commented that one of the planes made it home after a collision with high-tension wires that tore one engine completely off the wing. Another plane, riddled with shellfire, bounced off the water during an aborted ditching attempt before successfully returning to base. The army manual ended its introduction by promising, "You will find it a pleasure to fly."

Often overshadowed by the Douglas C-47, Curtiss' C-46 Commando was a bigger machine that could fly farther and faster than its stable mate. The Commando was another civil passenger design, the CW-20, drafted into service by the army and navy. With the Japanese in Burma, the airplane that was ungraciously nicknamed "The Whale" and "Dumbo" carried supplies from India to China over the treacherous Himalaya Mountains. Known as "the Hump," the route held some of the most unforgiving terrain and most extreme weather in the world, and cost the lives of some 800 U.S. airmen. But from April 1942 until August 1945, the 650,000 tons of supplies that flowed over the Hump helped keep China fighting in the war against Japan.

A Curtiss C-46 Commando of the 313th Troop Carrier Group takes off from Achiet, France, loaded with paratroopers. The plane was taking part in Operation Varsity, the massive airborne assault over the Rhine near Rees and Wesel, Germany, on March 24, 1945. *National Archives/Army Air Forces*

On November 13, 1943, a B-25 Mitchell dubbed *Ricardo* slid off the icy runway at Alexai Point on the island of Attu in the Aleutians. The following day, under similar freezing conditions, a C-47 locked up its brakes while landing and crashed into the bomber, causing major damage to both aircraft. No one was hurt in the accident. *National Archives/Army Air Forces*

This C-46 of the 313th Troop Carrier Group was damaged in Achiet, France, on March 24, 1945. Loaded with paratroopers of the 17th Airborne Division set to deploy near Wesel, Germany, this Commando veered off the runway during takeoff, flattened two jeeps, and hit this truck before lurching to a halt. Four paratroopers were injured in the accident. *National Archives/Army Air Forces*

When a Thirteenth Air Force C-47 became stranded in the brush at the end of a New Guinea jungle airstrip, a chief from a nearby village came to the rescue. Here, the men of his tribe drag the nine-ton cargo plane back to solid ground with sheer muscle power. The men regarded the event as a festive occasion, and many are wearing elaborate feather headdresses and necklaces. The Army Air Forces caption to the photograph adds, "Throughout New Guinea, the Dutch East Indies, and the Philippines, where the natives have been mistreated by the Jap occupation troops, airmen have encountered cooperation and help in emergencies." *National Archives/Army Air Forces*

A Chinese guard stands outside what can only be called a "unique" building at the 1338th Army Air Forces Base Unit in Yunnanyi, China. This derelict C-46, minus wings, has become "Hump Haven" for the men involved in flying the Himalaya Mountains—called "the Hump" by airmen. American soldiers based in faraway lands have always been an ingenious bunch. In this case, they figured if they needed to be working around the globe in China, the least Uncle Sam could do was to provide a classy-looking office building. This photo was taken in January 1945. *National Archives/Army Air Forces*

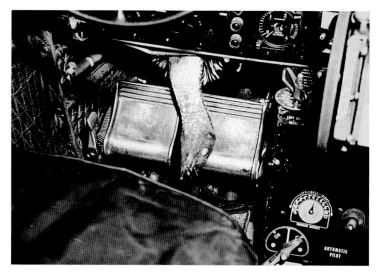

At 7,000 feet over Calcutta, India, the crew of this C-47 got a surprise it wouldn't soon forget: the plane smacked into a high-flying vulture. While hitting a bird isn't particularly uncommon, hitting one at that altitude is pretty rare. It's much rarer still when the bird is tough enough to rip though the nose and end up dangling between the pilots' knees. Pilots say that hitting a bird this size is nearly like being hit with a cannonball. *National Archives/Army Air Forces*

These C-46 Commandos were damaged in a typhoon that ravaged the aircraft at the 20th Bomber Command base at Kalaikunda, India, on March 12, 1945. The C-46 in the background was gashed through the tail by a tumbling Stinson L-5 liaison plane during the storm. *National Archives/Army Air Forces*

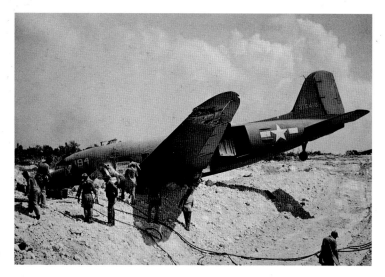

This C-47 ran off the runway at Angaur Island in the Carolines on October 23, 1944. Just weeks earlier, the small island had been under Japanese control. Attacked by U.S. Marines on September 17, the Japanese troops were beaten within three days. This C-47 was involved in bringing supplies to the island, which would serve as an airstrip for the 494th Bomb Group starting in November. Today, the corroded remains of a C-47, many B-24 bombers, and a navy Corsair fighter can still be seen on the island. *National Archives/Army Air Forces*

A mechanic looks for parts from a 315th Troop Carrier Group C-47 that appears to have nosed over during operations in Europe. "Standing on the brakes," as pilots called it, could cause a "trail-dragger" aircraft to flip up onto its nose, ruining the engines and propellers. *Military History Institute/Koerner Collection*

A 1st Troop Carrier Group C-47 encountered a Zero over the Pacific. After the Japanese fighter had expended all of its ammunition on the retreating Douglas aircraft, the frustrated fighter pilot decided to crash into the C-47. But the sturdy cargo craft flew on, amazingly landing safely with a "ventilated" fuselage. *The Boeing Company Archives*

American soldiers climb aboard a Waco CG-4A during invasion exercises. The CG-4A could carry 13 fully equipped troops. *Military History Institute/Milne Collection*

Silent Wings

Imagine guiding a heavily loaded glider in for a crash landing amid a blackened landscape dotted with trees, telephone poles, and stone walls. There was no turning back and no second chances for these "suicide jockeys" flying in fragile wood, metal, and fabric machines cheerily called "flying coffins" by GIs. The potential for disaster was enormous.

American airborne assaults in Europe and Burma used towed gliders carrying troops and equipment, along with paratroopers dropped from cargo planes, to surprise and confuse enemy troops and cut off enemy forces behind the front lines. For many combat glider soldiers, surviving the controlled crash was considered half the battle. Once their feet were on the ground, they felt that at least their lives were back in their own hands.

Airborne casualties were terribly high, and glider soldiers complained bitterly because they earned no flight pay or jump pay. Army officials believed that glider training and combat landings were much safer than jumping from a plane. As a glider infantry song from the time protests:

> We glide through the air in a tactical state,
> Jumping is useless, it's always too late.
> No chute for the soldiers who ride in a crate,
> And the pay is exactly the same.

Even after tragic accidents and frightening crashes during early operations proved that the gliders were, indeed, very dangerous, glider infantry received half the hazard pay of their paratrooper comrades.

The most widely used U.S. troop and cargo glider of the war was the Waco Aircraft Company CG-4A Hadrian. Soldiers who flew it generally referred to the plane as the Waco. Each cost the army $24,000 and could carry 13 fully equipped troops or a jeep, howitzer, or quarter-ton truck. Often, there were not enough trained glider pilots to man each of the

Waco's dual controls. Before flight, the lone pilot assigned to the craft would try to spot the most intelligent-looking infantry man. Placed in the copilot's seat, the shanghaied soldier would receive basic flight and landing instructions in case the pilot was killed or disabled during the flight.

Another glider used by U.S. forces was the British Airspeed Aviation Company's Horsa. Built almost completely of wood, the Horsa was bigger than the Waco, holding up to 25 troops. American flyers and soldiers preferred the Waco to the British glider because the CG-4A was slower, smaller, and lighter—all traits that could keep you alive while searching for the best place to set down. But many Horsas were flown into battle by U.S. forces, most notably in the early morning hours on D-Day, June 6, 1944.

St. Louis–based Robertson Aircraft Company was one of 15 manufacturers that made CG-4As during the war. On August 1, 1943, thousands of people turned out to see a demonstration of a Robertson glider over Lambert Field. During flight, the CG-4A's starboard wing folded up and ripped free from the aircraft at an altitude of 2,000 feet. All 10 people aboard the glider were killed in the crash, including St. Louis Mayor William Dee Becker. Investigators found that the accident was caused by the failure of the wing-strut fitting, supplied by a local coffin maker. The fitting had been mistakenly machined much thinner than had been called for on the manufacturer's plans. *St. Louis Mercantile Library at the University of Missouri-St. Louis*

Airborne troopers inspect a cracked-up Horsa glider of the 9th Air Force Troop Carrier Command used in Operation Neptune. The photograph was taken somewhere in France after D-Day, June 6, 1944. Note that the censor has blanked out the soldiers' shoulder patches. *Peter Bowers Collection*

This Waco skids to a stop during a demonstration at Laurinburg-Maxton Army Air Base in North Carolina. "A few moments later," says the army's facetious caption about the lake landing, "Fifth columnists had supplied the glider with buoys and airborne infantrymen were making their way to shore to do their part in the invasion." *Peter Bowers Collection*

Horsa gliders used by American forces lie where they fell on the fields of France. Of particular interest are the spattered and hastily painted invasion stripes on these aircraft. It should be noted that even though these aircraft sustained major damage on landing, the gliders often were pulled apart after the fact. It appears that troops have dug into the side of the glider on the left to retrieve some piece of equipment that it carried. *Military History Institute/Gavin Collection*

Glider troopers loved to snap photographs of themselves with the most mangled and mashed machine they could find. Here, soldiers pose with totaled Waco CG-4As. These images were found in two soldiers' collections at the Military History Institute. The Waco on the right appears to have suffered a blast from a mortar round or grenade that shredded its tail. *Military History Institute/Knox and Galvin Collection*

A Waco CG-4A rests partially in a tree near Rees and Wesel in Germany on April 1, 1945. The glider was used in Operation Varsity, the massive airborne attack across the Rhine River on March 24, 1945. Thankful to be on the ground alive and intact, glider troops have long ago spilled out of the door under the Waco's wing and gone about their duties. *National Archives/Army Air Forces*

Gliders were not only used in Europe. During Operation Thursday, this First Air Commando CG-4A crashed near a landing site code-named Broadway in Burma. Chosen to avoid contact with Japanese ground forces, the site was located in rough and remote terrain. Trees and ditches at Broadway caused the crash of many gliders. Thirty men were killed and dozens more wounded in the first wave of landings on March 5, 1944. *National Archives/Army Air Forces*

Brakes and spoilers were not enough to keep this Waco CG-4A combat glider out of a line of barbed-wire fencing upon landing. The main wheels under the wings of the glider appear to have given way. Barely discernable, the fitting name *Sad Sack* is chalked on the side of the craft where the fence line meets the fuselage. *Stan Piet/Army Air Forces*

A young boy in Washington State had a heck of a story to tell his schoolmates after this Stearman PT-17 Kaydet fell into his backyard. The McChord Field–based trainer plowed through pine trees, lost its engine as it crunched over the top of a shed, and came to rest next to the family's jalopy. It is not clear if the flyer, or flyers, in the aircraft survived the accident. *The Museum of Flight/Langmack Collection*

Learning to Fly

Almost 25 percent of aircraft accepted by the army during the war were trainers. Critical to the education of the pilots who would fly the fighters, bombers, and cargo planes into battle, training aircraft were used (and often abused) stateside in the effort to teach flyers everything from the fundamentals of flying to the complexities of military formations, aerobatics, and combat tactics.

Flight training was divided into primary, basic, and advanced courses. A prospective pilot might start training by going aloft in a rugged and simple Stearman PT-13 or a Ryan PT-22 with an experienced instructor. In the approximately 60 hours of flight time over the nine weeks of primary training, students learned to handle an aircraft and would take their first solo flights.

Airmen who passed all of the courses in primary would move on to a heavier and more powerful aircraft, such as the North American BT-9 or Vultee

BT-13, in basic training. This intermediate step in training usually took another nine weeks and taught each man formation flying, night and bad-weather flying while relying on instruments, and navigation on cross-country flights.

With about 70 more hours under his belt, the flyer then could move on to advanced training. Future fighter pilots might operate a plane such as the North American AT-6 while perfecting gunnery and air-combat tactics, while those chosen to fly multi-engine machines would polish their skills in a plane such as the twin-engine Cessna AT-17.

During the war, more than 3,500 air cadets lost their lives, and countless more were involved in accidents while working to become pilots. As a prospective flyer continued his flight training, his chances of dying in an accident increased because the curriculum became more difficult and the aircraft he flew became bigger, more complex, and much less forgiving of mistakes. During the war, primary training claimed 439 lives, basic took 1,175, and advanced stole 1,888 from the pool of U.S. Army and Navy pilots being trained to fight overseas.

Most accidents in training were fairly common and minor. As young men learned to master their new trade, there were hundreds of taxiing collisions, smashed propellers, ground loops, and nose-overs. The student would emerge with only his ego damaged, an angry instructor, and a valuable lesson learned. Much to the fledgling pilot's chagrin, some curious bystander was almost always nearby with a camera to record, for all time, the results of the student's bungle.

The pilot of this North American BT-9 was killed when the plane stalled on landing at Krueger Field, Texas, before the war. When the flying cadet realized he was going to undershoot the runway, he gunned the engine and pulled up hard. The trainer stalled and fell to the ground. These photos were taken on May 4, 1937. *Air Force Historical Research Agency*

Prospective pilots gather around an instructor and a North American basic trainer at Randolph Field in Texas. Known as "The West Point of the Air," Randolph was named after Air Corps Captain William Millican Randolph, who died in an AT-4 crash in 1928. Strangely, William Randolph was on the committee to name the new field when he was killed. *National Archives/Army Air Forces*

A fuel-switching problem grew into a forced landing for the pilot of this Fairchild PT-19B. With only 30 hours in the air and no experience in this type of aircraft, the pilot took off to ferry this trainer from Middletown, Ohio, to East St. Louis, Illinois, on September 7, 1943. He didn't make it too much farther than the end of the runway. Fuel was found in the lines between the tank and the selector valve, but none was present from the valve to the engine. "Such error is considered by the board to be carelessness," the accident report says. *Air Force Historical Research Agency*

This sharp-looking PT-17 was flipped over at Wright Field, Ohio, by a strong gust of wind while taxiing downwind at 10 miles per hour on April 2, 1943. That gust, which the pilot estimated to be nearly 30 miles per hour, lifted the tail off the ground. "When the tail lifted," says the flyer in the accident report, "throttle was used in an attempt to bring the tail down, but was not effective." *Air Force Historical Research Agency*

This Stearman PT-17 ended up buried in the woods near McChord Field in Washington. No one envied the person who was ordered to take this plane apart and haul it out of the trees to the nearest road. *The Museum of Flight/Langmack Collection*

The unlucky pilot of this Stearman PT-13 explains the damage to his plane as such: "I had just completed my fourth landing and was just rolling to a stop when another plane came in for a landing on my left side and landed on my left wing, smashing the upper left wing and twisting the lower left wing and turning the other plane over on its back. No injury to personnel or damage to private property." The incident happened at Davenport Field, Texas, on April 5, 1937. *Air Force Historical Research Agency*

This North American AT-6 Texan was tripped up at Rosecrans Field near St. Joseph, Missouri. The gouge in the foreground shows where the plane nosed over, dug in, and flipped during a landing on April 18, 1945. *National Archives/Army Air Forces*

This Stearman PT-17 became the victim of an unusually fierce hail storm at an unknown location in the United States. The plane will need reskinning before it will be used again in training. Note the unusual Morse code "dot dot dot, dash" (or "V") below the serial number on the tail. *Peter Bowers Collection*

A young lieutenant plowed the fields the hard way with his grasshopper on December 30, 1942. The plane, named *Miss Denver*, came down in Keevil, England, the home of the 62nd Troop Carrier Group. *The Museum of Flight/Dyche Collection*

Grasshoppers

During military maneuvers in 1941, Major General Innis Swift gave army liaison planes their nickname. After watching an olive drab–painted light plane lurch to a stop after a rough landing in a bumpy field, he happily exclaimed to the pilot, "You looked just like a damn grasshopper when you landed that thing out there in the boondocks and bounced around." Soon, all liaison planes were called grasshoppers.

Though initially unsure that an unarmed and unarmored plane could survive in a battle area, the army accepted 13,558 liaison-type aircraft into its inventory between June 1940 and August 1945. More than 65 percent of these were military versions of the Piper Cub, called the L-4, and the Stinson 105 Voyager, called the L-5.

Grasshoppers didn't capture one's imagination like the sleek fighters and formidable bombers slugging it out in the heavens above. Often unrecognized and unknown, liaison planes and their pilots had an intimate relationship with the soldiers on the ground because they were "beating the bushes" and "peeking under rocks"—always helping to look for enemy activity.

It was said that when a grasshopper was in the area, the Germans moved nothing but their eyeballs for fear of attracting attention to themselves. Though the puddle jumpers were unarmed, being caught in the open by one meant bad things were soon coming your way. Within minutes, a radio call from the simple machine could bring a heavy rain of artillery fire. When not scouting the countryside or directing artillery barrages, grasshoppers were used as couriers, flying messages and high-ranking officials from place to place.

Aware of the grasshoppers' unique importance on the battlefield, enemy troops and pilots sometimes received special rewards if they could bring one down. Cruising slow and low, grasshoppers often were hounded by enemy ground fire and hunted by fighters. The trick to staying safe when an enemy fighter plane attacked was to make a series of hard right turns while hugging the ground. With these tactics, a faster and less maneuverable hostile aircraft had trouble bringing its guns to bear on a skillful pilot and his little light plane.

Springing aloft from only yards of real estate and making a power-stall landing in even fewer, grasshoppers could operate from the strangest places—cow pastures, beaches, or small stretches of roadway. Liaison planes commonly came to earthly grief when their pilots misjudged their surroundings.

Many a grasshopper ended life in a water-filled shell hole, entangled in a barbed-wire fence, or bashed by a telephone pole or tree stump that was seen a split second too late.

Soldiers load out a Piper L-4 grasshopper on the shore of a Pacific island. The little grasshoppers were critical to the fighting here and in Europe, scouting the enemy and directing artillery.
Military History Institute/Milne Collection

This Stinson L-1A Vigilant couldn't move fast enough to dodge a tree near an airfield in central Burma. The pilot and three infantrymen were rescued by soldiers with the help of ladders, ropes, and pulleys. The pilot, Sergeant W. H. Latta, painfully makes his way down from the wreck in the image to the right. He suffered a fractured leg and lacerations to his face. *National Archives/Army Air Forces*

This photo shows two of the many planes damaged by a typhoon on March 12, 1945, at the 20th Bomber Command base at Kalaikunda, India. Lighter aircraft, like these Stinson L-5s, were thrown about by the gusts. Note a third L-5 is overturned in the background. *National Archives/Army Air Forces*

The pilot of this Piper L-4J was dodging gunfire from an attacking German Bf 109 when he lost control. His flight ended in a haystack in Germany, where soldiers of the Fifth Armored Division worked to free him from the liaison plane's wreckage. *National Archives/Army Air Forces*

This Stinson L-5B fell during the fighting for the island of Okinawa between April and June 1945. First it struggled back to the army's Cub Field No. 7 for a crash landing. Later and at another location, the very damp 163rd Liaison Squadron plane underwent recovery efforts in the rain. *National Archives/Army Air Forces*

This L-4 was flash-cooked when a stricken B-26 Marauder crashed to earth nearby. Though pulled from the fire, most of the plane is a loss. The skinless grasshopper gives an interesting look at the Piper's construction with its welded steel-tubing fuselage and aluminum wing ribs and leading edges. This accident happened on May 29, 1943. *National Archives/Army Air Forces*

This YP-80A Shooting Star crashed with Lockheed's chief test pilot Milo Burcham at the controls. The plane fell near the rim of a gravel pit in North Hollywood, California, after it took off from the Lockheed Air Terminal. Witnesses say the plane gained only 50 feet of altitude before the engine quit. Investigators found that the jet fighter's faulty overspeed governor caused the accident. *The Museum of Flight/Langmack Collection*

Stepping into the Future

Many new technologies came into their own during World War II. New systems such as the jet engine and radar would become integral parts of the military aircraft of the future. With amazing successes and a few heartbreaking failures, the Army Air Forces worked with scientists and aircraft companies to develop faster, stronger, and more effective aircraft than the Axis.

The system of radar (radio detection and ranging) was developed before the war and vastly was improved during the conflict. From land-based radar towers used in the Battle of Britain, to ship-mounted devices, to an arrangement small enough to fit into an aircraft, radar became smaller, better, and more powerful over months, not years, as the battles raged.

Delivery of production versions of the Northrop P-61 Black Widow started in late 1943. The plane was America's first specifically designed night fighter and carried an SCR-720 radar system in its nose. Snooping the night skies, the P-61 could slide behind an unsuspecting enemy, completely unseen. The Widow's prey often didn't know what was happening until bullets started crashing through his doomed aircraft.

Another invention that changed world of air warfare was the jet-propelled airplane. When the German Me 262 appeared, it could fly much faster than an American Mustang or Thunderbolt, causing a shudder among army pilots in Europe. But the lack of trained pilots, a shortage of fuel, and Hitler's insistence that the plane be used as a fighter-bomber rather than an interceptor kept Allied losses from jet attacks relatively rare.

Bell Aircraft Corporation developed America's first jet plane, the XP-59A Airacomet. When this fighter didn't live up to expectations, Lockheed Aircraft Company stepped in with the P-80 Shooting Star.

The P-80 design actually was field-tested in Italy during World War II, though none ever fired a shot during that combat. While the P-80 was a marked improvement over conventional propeller fighters, the transition to jets often was difficult for pilots. America mourned the loss of its all-time leading fighter ace, Richard Bong, when he died in a Shooting Star accident on August 6, 1945—just days before the end of the war.

Other successes and failures came and went from the army's ranks during the last years of the war. While an aircraft such as the Curtiss P-40Q signaled the end of a long line of Warhawk fighters, and the Curtiss XP-60 program never really got started, planes such as Lockheed's new Constellation airliner were drafted into military service, and Boeing's C-97 began a distinguished career that would last for many years to come.

A pair of Lockheed YP-80A Shooting Stars cruise near Mount Vesuvius in Italy. Brought overseas before the end of hostilities, the two jet fighters gave Air Forces personnel a preview of the air speeds and air wars of the near future. *National Archives/Army Air Forces*

A landing gear failure during a night landing on the island of Saipan damaged this P-61 Black Widow. The plane's crushed radome lies nearby as crewmen concentrate on the night fighter's SCR-720 radar system. This photo was taken on July 21, 1944. *National Archives/Army Air Forces*

Four P-61s returned to Iwo Jima as the sun came up on the morning of April 20, 1945. It was too foggy to land, so the pilots were instructed to orbit over the island. As fuel ran low, the tower talked the pilot of *Midnite Madness* (seen on the left) into the haze. The plane made it down safely—with only a blown tire. *The Spook* (seen on the right) was next, and the unlucky night fighter bounced once and came down right on top of the first plane. *The Spook*'s 20mm guns ran wild and fired until they ripped out of the plane's belly. Hearing the carnage happening below on the radio, the third Black Widow crew elected to bail out. The fourth aircraft had enough fuel to stay in the air until the fog had cleared. Luckily, the crews all survived the accident, suffering only minor injuries. *National Archives/Army Air Forces*

An army flyer near Van Nuys, California, got a shock when the engine on his Lockheed P-80A quit as he circled over the airfield. He made a belly landing and escaped the wreck unharmed. What he saw when he inspected the plane was sobering—there were two large holes in the fuselage where the turbine wheel was located and the wheel was completely gone. A similar failure had happened to test pilot Tony LeVier a few weeks earlier. In that instance, the jet fighter's tail had ripped completely off, leaving LeVier no choice but to use his parachute. Investigations found that the lower parts of the steel-alloy ingots that were used to make the turbine wheels were filled with impurities. Once only wheels produced from from the top half of the ingots were used, the problem disappeared. *The Museum of Flight/Langmack Collection*

The third Lockheed C-69 ran into trouble when the big plane's starboard main gear folded backwards during a taxi test at the company's plant at Burbank, California, on July 12, 1944. Corrections to the problem delayed the production program. The plane was one of many slated to become a civil airliner before the U.S. Army began to draft the planes right off the assembly line to be used as transports. The civilian interiors were replaced with 44 seats on the starboard side and four folding benches on the port side. *The Museum of Flight/Langmack Collection*

One of the army's XC-97s caught fire over Patterson Field, Ohio, on March 27, 1946. Like its predecessor, the B-29 Superfortress, the early versions of the C-97, and its new and powerful Wright engines had trouble with in-flight fires. In this case, there were no fatalities, though the pilot severely sprained his knee and the copilot fractured his wrist and wrenched his back when they jumped from the cockpit through the copilot's window. Note that the plane's serial number and the lettering on the nearby truck have been censored in the image. *Peter Bowers Collection*

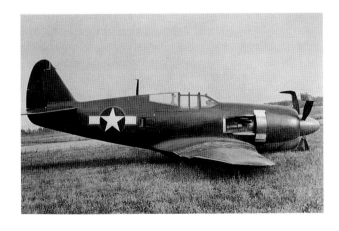

The P-60 series of aircraft went through many types of engines in attempts to come up with a winning combination. Packard Merlin, Allison, Pratt & Whitney, and even an experimental Chrysler 16-cylinder engine were tried in the plane. Here, the E-model, equipped with a Pratt & Whitney R-2800, lies in the grass after a belly landing. The army encouraged pilots, when they had a choice, to land on a runway instead of the grass because it caused less damage. "Dirt rolls up into balls, fracturing a plane's skin and rupturing the members," says a 1944 army publication. In this case, the plane's low-slung belly scoop has been completely torn loose and carried away in the crash. *Peter Bowers Collection*

The engine of this mud-spattered Curtiss P-40 lies torn from its mounts in a field somewhere in the United States. The fighter was ripped apart during a tumbling emergency landing. Note the insignia: After May 1942, the red center of the United States' national insignia was eliminated to avoid confusion with the Japanese insignia, called the Hinomaru. *The Museum of Flight/Stewart Collection*

Counting the Costs

From the attack on Pearl Harbor on December 7, 1941, to the Japanese surrender in Tokyo Bay on August 15, 1945, the U.S. Army lost 65,164 airplanes overseas and in the continental United States.

Fierce fighting in North Africa early in the war and the lesser-known but significant contributions made by airmen based in the Mediterranean took 10,612 dusty fighters, bombers, and cargo aircraft from the army's squadrons. The heavy fighting in the skies over Europe claimed 17,082 Army Air Forces (AAF) machines, peaking in the year 1944, when the all-out assault on German forces came at a price of 10,447 U.S. aircraft destroyed, worn out, or simply missing.

In the Pacific and the Far East, the island-hopping campaigns and the battles in the skies over Japan claimed 9,274 army planes shot down by enemy fighters or flak, stripped to nothing but skeletons, or sunk to the bottom of the Pacific Ocean.

The icy runways and bad weather in Alaska and its Aleutian Islands accounted for many of the 492 losses that the army suffered there, while combat with the Japanese claimed the rest. Support of the Chinese, fighting over Burma, and tough flying in the skies over India resulted in the loss of 3,289 more AAF aircraft.

Losses at faraway outposts such as Greenland, the Caribbean, South America, and Antarctica claimed 826 more AAF airplanes during the war. And then there were the painful losses of 23,589 airplanes at home. Warplanes fresh from the factory, which were being ferried into battle or employed at training schools around the United States, were not immune to accidents.

More important than the loss of aircraft, World War II claimed 121,867 battle casualties in the ranks of the Army Air Forces. A total of 18,238 men were wounded seriously enough in battle or in accidents to never return to the fighting. Furthermore, 63,568 more army airmen were reported missing, interned, or captured by the enemy. And 40,061 young American men died while flying and fighting for the U.S. Army.

An army pilot broods near the nose of his crashed P-38 after an emergency landing at Barakoma on Vella Lavella in the Solomon Islands on October 7, 1943. Though he has yet to put down his flying gloves or remove his Mae West life vest, the ammunition his plane carried is already being removed. *National Archives/Navy*

The 11-man crew of a 500th Bomb Group B-29 poses near the severed nose of its plane on Saipan. A propeller from the bomber spun off and ripped a gaping hole in the side of the plane while it was in flight. Upon landing, the Superfortress hit another B-29 named *Sky-Scrapper II* and broke in half. Miraculously, no one was hurt in the accident. *National Archives/Army Air Forces*

The muddy effects of an army navigator, set out on a parachute, were found in the wreckage of a bomber sunk 25 feet in a marsh near Zegveld, Holland. The man's dog tags, wallet, and navigator's wings helped identify which lost aircraft had been discovered. *Military History Institute/Milne Collection*

Radio operator Robert Hanson of the B-17F *Memphis Belle* kisses the ground after the *Belle* returned home from her 25th mission on May 17, 1943. The B-17 and her crew were the first of the 91st Bomb Group to complete 25 combat missions over Europe. *National Archives/Army Air Forces*

A seemingly endless pile of metal scrap stretches away from the camera on an unknown Pacific island. In layers, one can see LVT amtrac and M3 half-track vehicles used in the fighting to take the island. Near the top and foreground, air activities have added to the pile. A B-24 Liberator nose section and a B-29 Superfortress fuselage can be easily identified. *Stan Piet*

"I Wanted Wings"

— Composer unknown

I wanted wings 'till I got the goddam things,
Now I don't want them anymore.
They taught me how to fly and they sent me here to die,
I've had a belly full of war.
You can save those Zeros for the goddam heroes
'Cause distinguished flying crosses do not compensate
 for losses, buster.
I wanted wings 'till I got the goddam things, now I don't
 want them anymore.

I'll take the dames while the rest go down in flames,
I've no desire to be burned.
Air combat spelled romance: But it made me wet my
 pants,
I'm not a fighter I have learned.
You can save those Mitsubishis for the other sons of
 bitches,
'Cause I'd rather lay a cute thing than be shot down in
 a Mustang, buster.
I wanted wings 'till I got the goddam things, now I don't
 want them anymore.

I'm too young to meet my maker in a damned old
 Liberator,
That's for the eager, not for me.
I don't trust my luck to be picked up in a Duck,
After I have crashed at sea.
Oh, I'd rather be a seamstress than a sucker in a
 Fortress,
With my hand around a bottle, not around a throttle,
 buster.
I wanted wings 'till I got the goddam things, now I don't
 want them anymore.

I'm too old to learn new tricks in a B dash two crash six,
Blazing a path for Patton's tanks.
My wife don't want insurance and I'm not out for
 endurance,
I'd rather go to Paris and spend francs.
In England it was blitzes and in France it's
 Messerschmittzes,
Oh, I feel like such a sucker when my asshole starts to
 pucker, buster.
I wanted wings 'till I got the goddam things, now I don't
 want them anymore.

The day we bombed Metz, I ran out of cigarettes,
I always smoke to calm my gut.
They make them by the ton, but I haven't got a one,
I simply cannot fly without a butt.
Oh, the home front may be pitchin' but we still will do
 our bitchin',
'Til we find some real smart cookie that can
 mass-produce some nookie, lookie.
I wanted wings 'till I got the goddam things, now I don't
 want them anymore.

I don't want to tour over Berlin or the Ruhr,
Flak always makes me part my lunch.
I get no "hey hey" when they holler "bombs away,"
I'd rather be home with the bunch.
Oh, I'd rather come home buster, with my ass than with
 a cluster, buster.
I wanted wings 'till I got the goddam things, now I don't
 want them anymore.

(Just foolin')

Index